When I'm Dead All This Will Be Yours

JOE TELLER:
A PORTRAIT BY HIS KID
TELLER

CARTOONS, ILLUSTRATIONS,
& PAINTINGS BY
Joe Teller

BLAST BOOKS
New York

Blast Books gratefully acknowledges the generous help of Celia Fuller, Don Kennison, and Ken Siman.

Published by Blast Books, Inc.
P. O. Box 51, Cooper Station
New York, NY 10276-0051

ISBN 0-922233-22-5

DESIGNED BY LINDGREN/FULLER DESIGN

The text in this book is set in Cooper Oldstyle.

Printed in China

First Edition 2000

10 9 8 7 6 5 4 3 2 1

The Title

Joe Teller (my father—I call him "Pad" from the nonsense chant "daddy-paddy-boomeladdy") led me down the rickety cellar steps of my parents' nineteenth-century row house in Philadelphia.

Pad planted his eighty-seven-year-old, two-hundred-pound, six-foot-two body on a sawhorse beside the massive workbench he built forty years ago. Amber light from the bare hanging bulb reflected off his head, bald as a jellybean.

"So," I said, "we need an eighth-inch flathead screw to fix the oven door."

He surveyed the fifty-year accumulation of tools, defunct appliances, and dismembered furniture that lines the shadowy cellar walls, then thought for a moment. "I can tell you igzactically where to find one."

He pointed to a shelf on which a dozen old coffee jars were flanked by a threadbare army cot and a bent-wire 1950s stovetop toaster.

"In one of those," he said.

I spread a newspaper on the workbench and emptied the first coffee jar onto it. Hundreds of entangled open safety pins poured out, mingled with India-ink pen points and loose string. I rolled up the newspaper and funneled the contents back into the jar and then opened another: ball bearings, picture wire, a Mexican peso, and souvenir matchbooks from a vacation in the 1950s. The next: wing nuts, out-dated batteries, sticks of ossified chewing gum...

Pad tapped me on the shoulder and made a grand gesture sweeping the cellar walls. "When I'm dead," he said, "all *this* will be yours!"

Finding the Cartoons

MAM: *Pad has a discovery.*

KID: *Okay.*

PAD: *How does the Gettysburg Address begin?*

KID: *Four score and seven years ago...*

PAD: *That's enough. And how old am I?*

KID: *Eighty-seven.*

PAD: *How about that! I can't get over Abraham Lincoln giving my age!*

KID: *That's true.*

PAD: *It'll never happen again. Mammy missed it when it happened to her.*

KID: *Poor thing.*

I was lounging on the recliner in my parents' high-ceilinged, Lincoln-era parlor. I was happy, surrounded by the paintings my parents have made during the more than sixty years of their marriage.

I was reading the comics in the *Philadelphia Inquirer*.

Suddenly I felt a presence over my shoulder. It was Pad's bald head, saying, "Did you ever see *my* cartoons?"

"Cartoons?"

We sprinted up the four flights of spiral stairs—Pad's new pacemaker was doing its job—to the bare-plaster room at the top of the house, where Mam (short for "Mammy"—my mother, Irene) and Pad go each day to paint.

At opposite ends of the studio were, as ever, two works in progress, each with its own palette, easel, and canvas. Here: Mam's meticulous still life, silk flowers and sparkling cut glass. There: Pad's shrieking abstract, eye-searing prismatic colors slashed on the canvas with a painting knife.

Pad went to the rear of the studio, pushed aside the faded green plastic shower curtain that hangs in the doorway, and led me into the storeroom.

"Look up there," he said, pointing to the topmost of the deep home-made shelves full of unframed paintings jammed in like junk books in a Salvation Army thrift shop. I climbed up and rummaged among the canvases and soot. There I found a black portfolio, its rotting canvas flaps tied closed with twine. It was about the weight of an unabridged dictionary. "Howsabout *you* carry it down?" Pad said. "We'll show Mammy."

I lugged the portfolio downstairs to the kitchen table, where all matters of moment in my parents' house are unfolded. Mam was at the table, fervently studying the newspaper through her big oval eyeglasses. At the time she was ninety-one years old, but no important event (or incidental mention of her showbiz son) ever escapes her news-hungry eye. Seeing our need for exhibition space, she folded up her newspaper and wiped the green plastic flannel-backed tablecloth with a sponge.

I cut the gritty twine on the portfolio and lifted the decomposing cardboard cover. There, mounted on 14" x 18" mat boards, were more than a hundred cartoons.

Most were wryly observed scenes from Philadelphia street life. Adults on a subway bench self-consciously avoid touching one another, while kids in the foreground sleep cozily leaning on each other's shoulders. Two women gossip in the shadow of the enormous brass eagle in Wanamaker's department store. A bum preaches salvation to a fellow

"My dear, there are spies *everywhere.*"

"You're too meek. You're not inheriting anything."

bum outside a church. A window washer is skinnier than his squeegee pole. A too-affectionate drunk scares the bejeezus out of a young woman while a subway cop looks on indifferently. A naughty child chops up the dining room furniture.

Some were downright surreal: a burglar is caught by a nightmarish gorgon of a woman in curlers. Two dogs dressed as dames walk a man on a leash.

Some had captions, but in most the delight was all in the drawing.

"You drew these?" I said to Pad. Now, I knew about his painting and sculpture and commercial lettering design. And I'd enjoyed the funny drawings he makes on birthday cards. But I had no idea he had pursued cartooning so seriously.

"Sure I did," he said.

I pointed to the credit line at the top of one drawing. "It says, 'Town Tunes—by Tipsy'! Who's Tipsy?"

"They ain't got but the five bucks in the cookie jar!"

"Now be careful! This is your good coat!"

"Stop whistling—you'll wake the baby!"

"I guess I wanted a name that sounded like Lichty—George Lichty. He drew 'Grin and Bear It.' I liked the way he made those cartoons swing so free and easy-like."

Mam fingered her creamy white hair, remembering. "We were living on Spring Garden Street then. You drew them right around the time we were married."

"April fourteenth, nineteen-thirty-nine. A day that will live in infamy," Pad declared. Mam laughed.

"Were they ever published?"

"'Many a flower was born to blush unseen and waste its sweetness on the desert air,'" Pad said.

"Isn't that the truth!" said Mam. "You didn't get that from *The A-Team*, did you?"

"No, it's…my father used to recite him to us kids…Thomas Gray. Now how the hell did I remember that?"

"Are you sure?" said Mam. "You're liable to get *anything* from *The A-Team*…"

Like Proust,
But Shorter and with Pictures

MAM: *The problem is we live too long. We're alive too long for what our bodies can do. They simply wear out. The sensible solution would be just to take your own life when it's time. But you can't do that if you have a famous son—it would be bad publicity.*

Finding Pad's cartoons was thrilling.

It was also unsettling.

In those cartoons I saw images from the decades my parents had lived before I made my late entrance (my mother was nearly forty when I was born). As I looked at them I realized I knew nothing about nearly half of their lives.

Sure, I could have told you that Pad's parents were from Russia, that he played Tarzan on a trapeze in the woods of Fairmount Park when he was a boy. I knew Mam had lived on a farm and met Pad in art school. And I'm aware that Mam and Pad are locked in a mysterious, titanic love that is somehow linked to art.

But to me their early lives were a frustrating murk of overheard names and places: Yappy, Clayton, County Line, Colonnade, Graphic Sketch Club, Camp Hahn.

So why had they told me so little about their past?

"But he won't need another pair of pants
until he goes to high school."

If you walk into my parents' house, the answer is obvious. Aside from their most recent paintings, there is nothing hanging on the plaster walls but their Kid. No portraits of their ancestors. No snapshots from their travels. Just the Kid. Photos of the Kid starring as George Washington in a fifth-grade school show; reviews of the Kid opening on Broadway; stills from his first appearance on *Saturday Night Live*.

When Pad and Mam became parents, they decided that everything that had gone before was an insignificant prologue to the big event: launching a human life.

That's ideal for a child, of course. But now I'm more than fifty years old and starting to smell the past in the present. To have at my elbow for who-knows-how-much-longer the two most intriguing individuals in my cosmos and never to ask them to tell their story—well, that would be really, really dumb.

I visit my parents about once a month, stay for several days, take them on little excursions in a rented car, unclog the vacuum cleaner. And when I'm not visiting, I call them every evening. So, I reasoned, why not *use* the opportunity? At first I felt a little awkward. It seemed rather like probing under the sheets where I had been conceived.

But once they realized I loved what they were telling me, their memories began to pump and the stories flowed. And now when I look at the cartoons, I am no longer unsettled. I see the funny, dramatic, romantic world Joe and Irene lived in before their little Bundle of Joy transformed them into Mam and Pad.

And they're happy, too, knowing that when they're dead, all this will be mine.

Snakey

A lady called today. She said, "Mr. Joseph Teller?"
I said, "Uh-huh."
She said, "I'm calling from Laurel Hill Cemetery."
I said, "Oh, my goodness. Are you dead?"
She said, "Not all of us are dead. Some people work here."
She was trying to sell us cemetery plots, but I told her we
  already made our preparations for our departures from
  this world. We had a very pleasant conversation and I
  said, "Call again, any time."

I

Mam started her dinner at eight in the morning.

She unwrapped and washed a fresh loin of pork in the kitchen sink where she had once bathed me. Then she lovingly rubbed the pink flesh with salt, pepper, garlic powder, and poultry seasoning. She bejeweled the pork with little onions, pinning the half-bulbs all over the outside with toothpicks to baste the meat during roasting. Finally she nestled the pork in a black enameled pan, clamped on the lid, and set it in the oven at 350 degrees.

While the meat was cooking, Mam mounted the steep spiral stairs to the fourth-floor studio and worked on her current painting, a still life of flowers arranged in a vase that once had sat on her mother's mantel. Mam was trying to capture the effect of light on cut glass. Pad had argued it's impossible to re-create the effect in acrylic paint, but Mam simply said, "I know. I know. But I'm going to try *just* a little more before I give up." She'd been at it for four months.

Two hours later, Pad yelled up the stairwell, "Hey, Mama! Should I turn the meat off?" Mam washed her brushes in the coffee jar full of water and descended to the kitchen to check the pork. In any competition between food and art, food always wins if the artist is a mother with her grown son visiting for dinner.

II

The roast slept snugly in the oven with the heat off for the next three hours.

Pad hunched his big shoulders over the kitchen table. Cheerfully and with little regard for melody he sang "Jeanie with the Light Brown Hair" as he minced olives, peppers, lettuce, and tomatoes with a huge white ceramic knife, a beautiful tool whose indestructible edge fascinates him. He garnished his mincings with pimientos, and stuck them into the refrigerator, which he calls the "ice-a-box."

At two-thirty Mam fired up the oven again for the final browning. While Pad shucked the corn, Mam methodically carved sand pockets out of the fat asparagus spears and dissected the acorn squash into hemispheres, which she filled with brown sugar and margarine and put into the second oven above the pots bubbling on the four gas burners. By dinnertime, four o'clock, the heat was—well—infernal.

Mam dished up with an eye to color. The yellow corn was set off by a grass-green bowl. The green broccoli was complemented by a deep maroon platter. I was permitted the honorary role of carrying the ten or twelve steaming dishes to the table and setting them on the two dozen hotpads and trivets strategically placed to protect the flannel-backed plastic tablecloth.

Now, in the above account of the food preparation I've omitted (out of consideration for hungry and impatient readers) descriptions of the carrots, zucchini, lima beans, stewed tomatoes, and Italian sausage-noodle casserole. I've also not mentioned the pickles, coleslaw, and hot snowflake rolls, which in Mam's view don't count because they were bought ready-made.

Gazing on that monumental dinner was like looking down on Rome from an airplane window.

III

Mam offered dessert, but none of us was ready to face the dark-chocolate-shaving-covered hazelnut cake Pad fetches from the nearby Swiss bakery when I come to town. So I said, "All right, what chores can I do for you this visit? Repaint the numbers on your front door? Change the batteries in the smoke detectors?"

"Do you think you could lift that onto the kitchen table?" Mam pointed to a gray file box crammed behind the tea wagon in a corner of the kitchen. "Don't hurt yourself. It's heavy."

It was made out of some fireproof material that looked—and felt—a lot like cement. It sank into the tablecloth. If you were to lift this tablecloth, by the way, you'd find another flannel-backed plastic tablecloth of a different pattern (for, say, a holiday meal) and under that another and another, for—I swear I am not exaggerating—twelve layers, recording the history of my family's dinners like strata of the earth's crust.

"That box has everything," Mam said. "Birth certificates, marriage licenses, deeds, wills. We took them out of the safe deposit box. Our bank keeps changing its name and getting bought by other banks run by crooks who get paid a million dollars for getting fired, and they never tell us till the bank's sold and all our account numbers are changed. It's disgusting. Anyway, if you're not too sweaty to put those papers in some kind of order, that would certainly set my mind at rest."

I unpacked the strongbox onto the table. There were empty file folders and assorted old documents. While Pad washed and Mam dried the dishes, I read each document, put it in a folder, and labeled it. I stopped, puzzled, when I found a birth certificate for Israel Max Teller, born May 15, 1913, which is Pad's birthday.

"Did you have a twin brother who died?" I called to Pad.

"No," Mam interjected. "Just three older sisters who wanted to murder each other."

"So who's Israel Max Teller?"

"That's me," said Pad. "They called me Maxie all through elementary school. But when I got out into the world, I started calling myself Joe. It was my father's name and easy to remember."

How curious, I thought. When I went into the show business, I legally dropped my long-unused first name. Name changing must be in the genes.

IV

I knew Pad's father, Joseph Teller, Sr., as Pee-Pop, a handsome, upright old man who always dressed in a vested suit and tie and sat me on his lap to listen to the ticking of his gold pocket watch. Pee-Pop loved big words (*salubrious* was a favorite) and spouted quotations from Shakespeare and *Hatha Yoga*.

When he was a widower in his seventies he moved to California, whence he sent my family monthly packages crammed with books of old English poetry and loaves of preservative-free (and therefore moldy) "health" bread. I noticed that the return address on the packages changed frequently and asked Pad why. He said Pee-Pop's great vice

"That's *not* my inseam!"

was reading; he liked to buy used magazines and books, read them, stack them in his apartment until it was too full to live in, then move.

While my parents put away the dinner dishes, I sat examining my grandfather's immigration records. On the 24th of December 1900 Joseph Teller, age twenty-one, a native of Russia, was declared a United States citizen.

"My parents met in a Brooklyn garment factory," said Pad, drying his hands with a terry cloth towel I had lately persuaded him was more absorbent than the old undershirts he had been using.

Mam paused in her wrestling match with a stack of bowls on a shelf too high for a five-foot-tall woman to reach. "Your father could sew? I don't believe it!"

"My father was good with a sewing machine," said Pad. "He was a whiz making shirts. And my mother cut patterns. In the Old Country everybody learned a trade."

Joseph the shirtmaker married Esther the pattern cutter and they moved into a Jewish tenement, where they had four children: Eva, Clara, Ethel, and finally the only boy, Israel Max, whom they all called Sonny.

"Pop didn't like the garment business," said Pad. "All he really cared about was his literature. He read Hebrew and knew all the classic Yiddish authors."

"And Shakespeare, too," said Mam.

"English was tops for him. You pretty much couldn't name a subject without him busting out with some line from *Hamlet*. He knew Milton, Keats, Shelley—all the big guys—and he liked Americans, too: Longfellow, Whitman, Mark Twain. He grabbed any chance he could to get educated. He even went to night school."

Around 1918, Joe, Sr., moved the family out of Brooklyn and into a little row house he rented in north Philadelphia (2414 North Stanley Street, if you're in the neighborhood). He took a job as a streetcar motorman on the swing shift.

"With four females in the family, I had to share a room with him," Pad recalled. "He used to get up at four-thirty in the morning to take the people to work. Then he'd come back to the house and read until he had to go out again to take the people home.

"People would come up and lean on the rail beside him while he was trying to drive the streetcar. And they'd gab and gab," said Pad. "He couldn't stand listening to all that crap."

"Poor thing—he was so polite," said Mam. "He didn't want to tell them to go away."

"So he started chewing raw garlic," Pad said. "Nobody bothered him after that.

"He liked one thing about the job: People on the streetcar left their newspapers behind. He'd pick them up and read them. At the end of the day, he was a well-informed citizen.

"Pop constantly talked about current events. Remember, these were the days of Will Rogers, when you were supposed to have strong opinions on politics. My father did. He used to go down to the Ethical Society and make speeches."

"What kind of speeches?" I asked.

"Ethical, I guess. I never went there. He also wrote letters to newspaper editors, and they were so classy, they were always published. Pop had an unabridged dictionary before anybody ever heard of such a thing. It was on its own stand—*its own stand!* My mother gave him hell for buying it."

"She was a tyrant," said Mam.

"When it came to education or culture," Pad continued, "she wasn't the least bit interested. She liked cooking and she was a real seamstress. She used to make dresses for a store downtown, and when she had a big order she'd tell you not to bother her because she was 'bizzy by clucks.'"

"'Clucks'?" I asked.

"Cloaks, dresses. She used to make dresses and ties for some of the fancy stores downtown. And if you bothered her while she was 'bizzy by clucks,' she'd zouse you."

"'Zouse'??"

"Whack you on the back of the head." He demonstrated, smacking the back of his bald dome and looking stunned. "All two hundred pounds of her!"

V

The kitchen was still hot when we had our dessert. I was surprised that the chocolate shavings on the hazelnut cake hadn't melted.

The Teller family: young Joe, old Joe, and Esther.
How'd you like to be zoused by her?

Esther—another view.

"Is this for fightin' or for losin'?"

"Nice, dining in a steam room," I remarked.

"You know what a Turkish bath is?" said Pad. "My father used to take me once or twice a week. There wasn't such a thing as hot running water in anybody's home, so you'd go to a Turkish bath. You'd go into a hot room and they'd give each person a bucket of soapsuds and a brush made out of feathers. You'd sweat, then soap yourself up, then you'd jump into a cold pool. Then you'd do it all over again. Then they'd give you a sheet and you'd wrap yourself up in it and lie on a cot and take a nap. It was heavenly. It cost fifteen cents."

"By now it'd be at least a quarter," said I.

Mam snorted. "More like twenty-five dollars!"

Pad looked off into space dreamily. "They had one on every corner. It was big business in those days."

"I bet it was a relief to get out of your house," said Mam.

"It was a nuthouse. Animals used to just wander in. Dogs and cats and rats and my sister Ethel's boyfriends. Every day she'd bring around a new 'playmate' and she'd bang out all the latest jazzy tunes on the piano for them."

"Which aggravated your sister Clara," Mam added.

"Clara had gone to *college*. She worked for a funeral director who was in love with her, and they'd take moonlight cruises in her canoe, the *Claire de Lune*."

"And that galled your sister Eva," said Mam, turning to me. "She was the oldest and had to help support the family, while Clara got to go to a fancy college and have boyfriends."

"Eva sure worked hard," said Pad. "She could take shorthand and type faster than you could talk. She was the assistant to the editor of the *Inquirer*. But then the damn music critic started giving her free tickets to the opera. Then she started buying the opera records and playing them all the time."

"And your father couldn't stand opera, could he?"

"My father was poetically inclined. He was nuts for *nice* music, like Mendelssohn and Fritz Kreisler. He had all the Red Seal albums. He thought opera was just a lot of rambunctious noise."

"I pity your father," said Mam.

"What about *me*? Eva didn't have a boyfriend, so I had to *go* to all the operas as her *date!*"

VI

Joe was happiest out on the streetcorner. "I had a bicycle with a siren on the front wheel. I used to zoom around like a maniac with that siren screaming."

"And now you blow your top," said Mam, "whenever a kid bounces a ball against the front wall of our house."

The one knitting is Joe's sister Ethel, who once got fired for distracting the male employees.

"I would go down the alley and whistle through my fingers and that would be the signal for the kids to come out. We all had skates, the old four-wheeled kind, and used to zoom up to Midvale Avenue to the library. We'd get all the Peter Rabbit books, the Tarzan books."

"You mean these urchins were literate?" I asked.

"Sure! They were all pretty good readers and they could do arithmetic, too. Me, I started elementary school when I was five and a half and graduated in the eighth grade."

"Did you get an allowance?"

"Mostly we worked for Al Chaplin. He had a fruit store. You'd sweep up and he'd pay you. Sometimes he paid with a bag of apples.

"And there was a candy store with a phone, the only phone in the neighborhood. The phone would ring and the owner would shout out, 'Go get So-and-So at twenty-four-thirty-six!' Then one of us would go get the person and they'd pay us a few pennies.

"But mostly we just lounged on the corner. We played soccer and baseball, with garbage cans and streetlamps for goals and bases. We played football—real tackle football—and I could snake my way in and out of the guys. So they called me 'Snakey.'

"And then there was Shooie—his father made shoes. And Leapy— he had the last name Leopold. And Yappy—his last name was Jaspan— he had one arm withered from infantile paralysis, but he was a tough little bugger who went around all winter without a shirt."

"Yappy had the most beautiful henna-red hair," Mam said to me. "You met him once when you were little. We were in the Horn and Hardart cafeteria and Yappy came up and introduced himself and I told him you were Joe's son. And he just stared at you like you were a rare orchid."

Pad continued, "And the three of us, Leapy and Yappy and I, we'd go out to Lemon Hill in Fairmount Park and we'd rig up ropes and trapezes and play Tarzan. And we'd fall and break something, but we'd heal

"It's just a fishing hole for dames."

"Here's your leg, Al! We're done with the baseball game."

"Or if we didn't, that was okay, too. I remember Al Barrett was sitting on the back of an ice wagon when a car went out of control and cut his leg off. But he got around real good on his wooden leg, and sometimes he left that off and just whizzed around on a crutch. He could swear better than any of us, too. See, to be a real person in our gang, you had to be able to string out a lot of cusswords. Talk like an Englishman, you weren't welcome.

"Duke was the big Saint Bernard dog that hung around with us. He used to chase cats and kill them just for fun. Duke's best friend was a kid named Mike. Duke just loved him. Mike used to masturbate Duke every afternoon, and, let me tell you, that dog had some kind of big wang, too."

"You never told me that, Joe!"

"Well, it's not nice to say to a lady. We all used to pee up the alley and I didn't tell you that, either."

VII

Second Floor—Did we hev excitement lest night in de houze, Mrs. Feitlebaum!——Was almost by us a calumnity!

First Floor—What was?

Second Floor—Hm! What was, she esks!! I tut what we'll gonna hev to call a nembulence!

First Floor—Iy-yi-yi-yi-yi-yi-yi-yi-yi!! WHAT WASS???

Second Floor—What was? Mine woister enemies shouldn't hev it! De baby ate opp all de pills!!

First Floor—Iy-yi-yi-yi-yi-yi-yi-yi!! DE PILLS! He ate opp????

Second Floor—Yeh; de pills. I was stending, pilling potatoes, und was falling on de floor de potato pills. Und he was cripping on de floor, so he ate opp all de pills!!!!

First Floor—De potato pills he ate!! Yi-yi-yi-yi-yi—— Und what did you did?

Second Floor—I ran queeck in de medicine chest, und I took out a box peels—und I gave him queeck a peel he should take. Und now he's filling motch better.

Milt Gross, Nize Baby, 1926

Pad—pardon me—Joe (alias Maxie, alias Sonny, alias Snakey) was thirteen the year humorist Milt Gross put out a 208-page book called *Nize Baby*, in which he presents comical conversations "overheard" in an immigrant Jewish tenement building. The dialogue is spelled phonetically; for example, "trick lock in de monnink" for "three o'clock in the morning." He illustrates his stories with cartoons.

Joe loved *Nize Baby*. "It wasn't like a Tarzan book; that was fantasy. Milt Gross was talking about the way people really were. And the drawings—he made it all look so simple. Making it look that simple—oh, that's so hard."

Milt Gross, Nize Baby, *1926*

Joe especially savored Gross's parodies of the beloved warhorses of literature, such as Longfellow's *Song of Hiawatha*. In Gross's version, Hiawatha's Yiddish grandmother spins a tale explaining the shadows on the moon as the consequences of a domestic squabble complete with rolling pins and hooch. "My father didn't think too highly of Milt Gross," said Pad.

When I gave Pad a copy of Gross's *Dunt Esk!!* for his eighty-fifth birthday, I opened the book to "De Raven," a parody of Poe. I read aloud this line from the passage in which the narrator worries that the spectral bird may be an alcoholic hallucination:

"Hibby-jibbizz!!—Hev I gottem??"

Without missing a beat Pad responded,

> *"Dot lest bottle, did it stottem?*
> *Look it seets on his Bleck Bottom—*
> *Seets a Raven on mine durr!!*
> *Seets dere und ripitts voibotim*
> *Opp above mine chamber-durr*
> *One woid spitches: 'Navermore.'"*

Go back and read it aloud a couple of times. You'll be so leffing.

Milt Gross, Dunt Esk!!, 1927

VIII

"There was a hobo who corner-lounged with us—Charlie Newhall. He used to tell us stories about his travels, how he rode the rails all over the country.

"That put ideas into our heads. See, the trains loaded with coal from Reading used to run through the park near us. So we started patronizing that railroad quite a bit. We'd hitch a ride up to Conshohocken and ride back on another train bringing a load into Philadelphia.

"Charlie Newhall gave us other ideas, too. He was s'phisticated," said Pad, slicking back imaginary hair. "He used to live with a variety of women—all the hustlers loved to take him in and feed him.

"When I was about thirteen, Charlie Newhall took us down to Callowhill Street for a good time. Freddy Wilson worked in a pornographic picture shop and let us in the shop and showed us all the dirty pictures."

Mam was agape. "I didn't even know they *had* pornographic picture shops in those days!"

"Sure they did. And then Charlie took us to this little hole-in-the-wall tattoo parlor. And that's where I got the little butterfly on my left thigh. That was the tryout. Then I got the snake on my left arm because I was Snakey. It cost fifty cents."

He held up his left biceps. The serpent in faded blue ink, familiar from my earliest memories, turned in on itself. "What did your parents think of your Snakey tattoo?" I asked.

"I don't think they ever knew," said Pad. "I always wore clothes around them."

"You thought about having it taken off," said Mam, "didn't you?"

"Only about a thousand times."

Though just now I thought he looked rather proud of it.

"About how old," I said, "was Charlie Newhall?"

"Oh, *old.*" Pad nodded. "He must have been around twenty-one."

"Double or nothing?"

The Road

MAM: *Oh, I've had such a day. I burnt the broccoli and then I put twice one ingredient into the cornbread and had to double the recipe.*
KID: *My computer crashed three times today.*
MAM: *Really? How about that! I wonder why.*
KID: *Well, you know we just had a full moon.*
JOE: *Oh, we get a lot of full moons around here.*

I

A honeycombed tissue-paper Thanksgiving turkey hung from a string thumbtacked into the acoustic-tile ceiling over the harvest-themed flannel-backed plastic tablecloth. I was carving the real turkey.

As I put a leg on Pad's plate, Mam said, "That's what Clayton served you when he was trying to get you off the vegetarian diet, Joe, wasn't it? A turkey leg? And it was so delicious you gave up being a vegetarian."

"Uh-huh. Clayton, he had it all planned out..."

I interrupted. "Wait a minute. Who *was* Clayton?"

"I met him in Santa Monica, California, when I was on the road. He married my sister Eva."

"What do you mean, 'on the road'?"

"Tramping. Hoboing. I was about seventeen or eighteen and I went to every one of the forty-eight states."

Mam added, "And he sent home letters and his sister Clara kept them all in a shoebox."

Pad rubbed the top of his bald head. "Why the hell would she save *those?*"

The shoebox of hobo letters weighed a little under ten pounds and resided in a cracked gray plastic bag on the bottom shelf of a bookcase on the second floor. Next to it were three beat-up copies of *The Happy Prince and Other Fairy Tales* by Oscar Wilde, which Pee-Pop had sent to my family over the years in his various packages stuffed with moldy bread. My parents do not throw away books. On the black marble mantel opposite the bookcase, crumbling plaster busts of Mam and Pad, sculpted by my father twenty years ago, watched my scavenging serenely.

I took the shoebox downstairs and unpacked it onto the kitchen table: 214 letters, postcards, and loose envelopes the color of wheat and smelling like *very* stale vanilla cookies. Over the next three nights I read each letter and postcard aloud to my parents. It took nine hours, and Pad seemed to like it almost as much as *The A-Team.*

Pad's letters were always jauntily legible. The handwriting of some of his friends…well, it even taxed the talents of me, a former schoolteacher. But as I got deeper and deeper into the hobo shoebox, I sank into the rhythm of the writing. The faded blue ink seemed to grow clear, and smudged scratchings in soft pencil spoke crisply and articulately once more.

II

In 1929 Joe was sixteen. He had a full head of black hair. His family still called him "Sonny," even though he now towered over them at 6'2" and 165 pounds of sinewy muscle. He was halfway through high school.

One Monday in June of 1929 Joe flunked a history test, and he and his pal Andrew Muldowny decided they had had enough of school. Inspired by Charlie Newhall's thrilling tales of trampdom, they boarded a streetcar and headed out to see the world.

"When we reached the end of the line," recalled Pad, "Andrew realized I wasn't joking and said, 'Maybe, I think, I'd better go home.' But I just kept going."

A week later Joe's mother, Esther, received this card from Charlotte, North Carolina:

> *Dear Mom,*
>
> *No doubt you were wondering why I didn't come home Monday. Well, it was like this: I got a ride with a man right into Washington, D.C., so I might as well see as much as I can while I have the chance. I am not telling when I will get home, so please don't worry. I had a job on a farm for two days and made $2.50. I have $7.84 left.*
>
> > *Your son,*
> > *Sonny*

In Washington he headed for the train yard and hopped boxcars to Florida. He rode south through swamps teeming with snakes and alligators. Then he turned around and rode north.

"I stayed on the train right on through Philadelphia," Pad said with a grin.

Fortunately the train was full of oranges, which comprised the whole of his diet for the next four days. When he reached the Canadian border, the border cops caught him and sent him home. He didn't touch an orange for months.

"It won't work for you. Nobody needs six *Inquirers*."

III

His thirst for adventure momentarily slaked by citrus, Joe went back to school and lasted a whole year. But by December 1930 Philadelphia was cold and bleak—the 1929 stock market crash had sent unemployment high and spirits low. From beyond the gray, frozen Schuylkill River Sonny heard sunny California calling.

He headed for the train yard.

In late December Sonny's family received a gilt-edged Christmas card of the three Wise Men following the Star; it bore no message, only a reassuring signature from their son, now in Michigan. A month later a more informative postcard arrived from Sweetwater, Texas:

> *Dear Mom and Gang,*
> *I've got a job here, but it ain't paying very much. I'll be*
> *here for about 2 weeks yet.*

At the kitchen table Pad grinned. "I was in jail for vagrancy. They were awful nice—they fed me and gave me a place to sleep, and all I had to do was a little gardening and cleaning up."

By February 1931 Joe was writing from balmy Los Angeles. He didn't have a job, but that didn't matter too much because

> *I'm surrounded by beautiful palm trees and lawns with*
> *squirrels and birds that will eat right out of your hand.*
> > *So long,*
> > *Sonny*

In April he drifted to nearby Santa Monica, where he was sitting on a park bench when he fell into conversation with a suave, golden-tongued Irish-American hobo five years Joe's senior.

Sonny wrote home that he had found a friend.

I have a buddy now that has finished college. He is of a very dramatic nature and we can't stop laughing while we are together as we observe the passing horde.

"Oh, Clayton was a pleasure to listen to," said Pad. "He was never at a loss for words. He had read all the classics and oh, boy, could he talk! He very seldom used any curse words—whereas the Stars and Stripes were always coming out of *me*."

I asked what Clayton looked like. Mam closed her eyes and described him. "He was slender and muscular with a big hawk nose, prominent chin and cheekbones, and a face that was always red. He looked like Richard Dix."

"I think he wanted to be a movie star," Pad said. "His last name was McFagan but he always called himself Clayton LaMarr."

"Isn't that a perfect name for a character in a book?" Mam said.

So that was Clayton.

"There were lots of rich people out there," said Pad. "We'd sit on the pier and chew tobacco. And when a rich person would come by with a white poodle, and the dog would lag behind, we'd spit tobacco juice on it."

Together they got jobs at the Miramar Hotel, a posh Santa Monica resort patronized by movie stars. Clayton nicknamed Joe "Hasty" from his trademark of moving in slow motion whenever he was told to hurry and taking long naps when he was supposed to be working.

"Clayton hung around the hotel where all the fancy people came, and he had a new girlfriend every other day. I used to stand outside the room while he'd be inside servicing them. They'd pay him, too. He was a gigolo."

"He had a wonderful voice," said Mam.

"He sure did. He liked me because I was quiet and liked to listen to him. Sometimes we slept out on the ground and he used to tell me stories until I fell asleep. Like a father or something..."

"Can you remember any of the—"

"Oh, if only I could remember one tithe."

IV

One day on impulse Joe and Clayton hopped a boxcar to San Francisco, then on to Sacramento and Reno. They were a team. "We used to go up streets—Clayton would take one side and I'd take the other. We used to ask for jobs and hope they didn't give us any. And give us a sandwich instead."

The two tough hobos called each other "Kull," a Claytonism derived from an archaic verb meaning "to cuddle an infant."

Wherever Joe went, he continued to write to his family and collected their letters at general delivery at the local post offices. When his family sent money, he sent it right back.

> *I am hereby returning the ten spot that you so graciously*
> *have rounded up for your dear brother, requesting and*
> *wishing no more of that line. In other words, I have*
> *become quite a gentleman tramp and am just beginning to*
> *enjoy life to its fullest.*

For the next three months he sent several picture postcards each week: star mansions, tennis courts, orange groves. He made it clear that he was no casual tourist.

*I have seen and been at all these places I have sent you in
picture form. That is, in my spare time. Got a new pair of
shoes, too.*

He had the thrill of seeing a movie shot and then later going to a
theater to see it.

*I was in San Mateo Saturday and seen Winnie Lightner
in "Gold Dust Gertie." That's the picture I seen her make
down at Huntington Beach about 5 months ago.*

But in July 1931 the heat got to him.

> *It's too hot to write and it's too hot to sleep and almost*
> *too hot to eat. Therefore I'm gonna be an Eskimo when I*
> *grow up.*

After seven months on the road, he was feeling homesick and a little guilty about worrying his family. So he headed home, leaving Clayton to provide for the women of California.

V

Joe returned to high school. He was adept at algebra and grew fond of Spanish; he even tried writing Spanish songs. His favorite course was mechanical drawing.

"We drew tools and even knew how to draw a screw in detail," said Pad proudly. "Then we learned to draw all the different parts of a house, and for a final class project we built a real house right there in the Gratz High School gymnasium."

Clayton, still on the road, frequently wrote to Joe.

> *Should you still harbor any beautiful fantasies in regards*
> *to vagabonding—by all means discard them immediately!*

Clayton loved giving advice as long as he didn't have to take it.

He offered a curious plan to help Joe to give up smoking. Joe tried it and replied,

> *Dear Kull,*
> *I have bought a bar of paraffin and am constantly*
> *chewing on it in a grand effort to break away from*

smoking. Your suggestion. Also I have a harmonica,
which I play during the intervals of chewing and biting
thumbs. I can play "The Turkey in the Straw" and
"Hinky Dinky Parley Voo." Anything for diversion.

Buenas noches, su cierto,
Hasty

"Nacherally," said Pad at the kitchen table, "Clayton himself never gave up smoking." When Clayton gave advice about reading, however, Joe listened.

Read Blake the Mystic—you remember, Barrymore's
favorite author. Blake writes as the wind in the chimney—
his thoughts become the songs we hear in this chimney—
the songs of life without the bondage of words. So do not
try to understand or comprehend him. Only try to retain
his influence, which is the finest thing in the literary
world.

Joe respected Clayton's passion for literature but sometimes found his florid writing style a bit much.

What the hell do you mean by—"you whom I blindly
revere exceedingly"? And "your sylph-like being"? Aw,
nuts.

Clayton often wrote about women:

Our dear Mary has informed me that she in company
with another companion has decided upon a life of future
rhythm gaiety dance and many escapades of d'amour and

*soon expects to sail for Honolulu where, so they feel, live
Eros and Bacchus, also countless Apollos who live only to
please and aid lonely girls that Life heretofore has been
quite delinquent in pleasing.*

Clayton even waxed eloquent when tapping his Kull for a few bucks.

*Am in quite a quandary at this moment and must look to
you for succor. You see, Hasty, I have my suitcase in hock
and with the wages I am receiving I am afraid it will be
impossible to redeem it in time to leave here next week as I
had planned.*

"Clayton working for wages!" Pad interrupted, slapping his thigh.

*So if you can send me a few dollars immediately, I shan't
apologize over this bequest. I can guarantee the return of the
loan on Tuesday of the following week—from Katherine.*

Adios, amigo
Clayton LaMarr

" 'From Katherine'!" said Pad. "Oh, that's Clayton all right. Money just wouldn't stick to him."

"Why did you bring him home?" asked Mam.

"I didn't bring him. I gave him our address so he could write to me. Then one day he just popped in and stayed till he married my sister Eva. My mother loved him. He could kid her—he was the only person who could—and I mean he never did a lick of work, so all he had to do was amuse her. He ate like a horse. And—hahaha—he even brought in some barbells and did weight training—right at our house. And Eva took a shine to him and—"

"—and she had the best income in the family—"

"So they got married for a couple of years. Until one day she found him in the boiler room with another woman, and they got divorced."

"He wanted to be a writer, didn't he, Joe? But he never sold anything."

"He was a door-to-door book salesman for a while, but he quit. It was too much like work. What a character! Once when he was living with us, he went out to west Philadelphia and tried to bum from the houses, until somebody recognized him!"

"So what happened to him?" I asked.

"After Eva divorced him, we lost track of him. He's probably dead now. I wonder if he's dead. Yeah, he must be."

The Social Security Death Index shows that Clayton McFagan died in 1977 in California, amongst the beautiful palm trees and birds that will eat right out of your hand.

VI

Right after his nineteenth birthday in May 1932, Joe disappeared in the middle of the night.

The first thing he bought on the road was a stack of prestamped penny postcards so he would be able to write every day regardless of his financial condition.

> *Dear Gang,*
> *I will be away for a few days. Please bring the 3 little*
> *books of mine back to the library.*
>
>

Buenas noches,
Me

"No more hamburgers for me! I dreamt I had a job."

It was longer than a few days. In July he wrote to his pal Yappy.

Dear Yappy,
Passed Rhode Island State Institution and watched them
make little ones out of big ones.

Snake

"Big ones?" I said to Pad at the kitchen table.
He smiled. "Rocks."
In July 1932 Joe left Boston ("land of beans") and went through Maine, determined to get into Canada this time, but, alas,

Dear Yap,
Tried to drop into Nova Scotia. Was deported and here
I'm is. Curse for me. Write at once and let me know if you
can do a one-hander yet.

"Here I'm is" was a catchphrase of movie comedian Stepin Fetchit, whose superlatively lazy film persona struck Joe as the perfect role model. "One-hander" refers to Yappy's longtime ambition to learn to do handstands on his one good arm.
Joe mastered the art of squeezing much effect into a short postcard.

The backwoods road is lined with French houses. The
people here are good and kind. Watched them skin a pig.

Somewhere along the way—he doesn't remember when or how—Joe became a vegetarian.

Goddamit! Got another job! Big shot summer hotel.
Carried out a lady's luggage—made ½ buck tip! Had an

*argument with the cook. Such a big strong boy and don't
eat meat! Geesus Crist, Joe!*

This trip's last message:

So, I finally got fired. Enclosed find net proceeds.

...written, of course, on a postcard.

VII

In May of 1933 Joe left his family a little note in Spanish on his night
table and he was off again. This turned out to be his last, longest, and
grandest trip.

He headed north. This time he got to see Niagara Falls before he
got deported from Canada for the *third* time. He turned west.

> *It was a hot and sultry day. I was washing my feet in a
> clear, rock-bottomed creek, during my noonday siesta, and
> a flock of water-spiders came snooping around, keeping a
> wary eye on my big toe. They said, "What's 'at?" I wiggled
> it a bit and they all scattered, but soon returned to keep
> me company.*

He observed life on the road with a cartoonist's eye.

> *I saw an adagio dancer hitch-hiker. He was wearing gym
> shoes and a red velvet jacket, blue cord breeches, a red pair
> of stockings and a blue velvet hat. He'd get way up on his
> toes when he'd ask for a ride and wave his hand grace-
> fully, high in the air.*

A heat wave made him think of Eskimos again, and he set his sights on Alaska via Chicago and Seattle.

"In those days," said Pad in the kitchen, "all the gangsters gave away food so's they'd look like nice guys. I remember standing in Al Capone's breadline. He was a real bastard, you know."

By June 1933 he was in Montana,

> ...out where the jack-rabbits play London Bridges with the steers, while the coyotes on the hill howl and make weird noises in the Bad Lands.

"You'd be hiking along and they'd screech and the hairs would stand up on the back of your neck," said Pad.

> Saw about 250 kids from New York that have come here to the reforestation camps. What a bunch! They were mostly all lean, wan, sallow, wide-eyed looking, all excited but trying to look as nonchalant as possible as they pass an Indian chief or cowboy.

From Seattle in June 1933 he wrote:

> So I will proceed with a queer coincidence.
>
> I was chopping wood for Mrs. Dale and worked up an appetite and a four-bit hunk. When I was through, she gave me some Christian Science literature.
>
> Then I go over to Mrs. Cohen's and have gafeelta feesh with red beets with rice pudding and salad and coffee and sliced pineapple. So I remark about the fish, "Just like old times!"

And she says, "You Jewish?" and starts giggling like a
monkey and then asks me questions about my family.
  And then I walk away. "Goot Yawntiff," says I.
  "Wait a minute!" she says and hits me up for half a
buck. These kikes! Outrageous.

Joe looked forward to letters from home. But letters from Yappy in
his scrunched handwriting and smeared pencil were a challenge.

I received all your letters and, after reading them over, I
decided I'd laugh now and decipher them later in the
quietness of my room. Maybe you're crazy.
  I've just spent my last cent for this card. I see Alaska
as a tiny bubble ready to break...

VIII

On June 14th Joe wrote from Vancouver, British Columbia, to tell
Yappy how he had sneaked into Canada.

Here I'm is. I caught me a passenger [train] out of Mt.
Vernon yesterday and landed here at one in the morning.
  There is a tank on the oil burners of the Great North-
ern. I snuck in there and held my breath as we passed the
immigration officers.
  When the engine made for the roundhouse, the brakie
threw the switch and I stepped almost into the arms of a
bull. He hollered, "Hey, there!" And, man, I never run so
fast.

"Bull" means police officer. It's the respectful precursor of "pig."

I made my first Canadian dollar yesterday. It was so big that I could hardly stuff it in my pocket. I was working for a Scotch lady, who worked hard as hell one day, and the next she'd get a heart attack. Also, she was cock-eyed.

Ever closer to Alaska, in the third week of June 1933 Joe wrote to Yappy from Prince George, British Columbia.

I'm on my way to Prince Rupert where, if things break my way, I'll be going to Hazleton with a pack full of chuck, a blanket, an axe, a knife, and some matches. There I expect to take the old overland trail up the Yukon to Dawson City. As far as I've heard, there are telegraph stations every forty miles, while the distances in between are full of grizzly bears and wildcats.

I'll walk all the way, about 500 miles. In Hazleton I'll have to pass the police who might not let me in, but I can sneak around them, I guess...

He watched Canada go by from the open door of his boxcar.

This morning, just as the sun came over the mountain, I stuck my head out the door of the car and witnessed the spectacle of snow glistening in the morning sunlight atop the highest peak in Canada, Mount Robson.

I could feel the thinness of the atmosphere. It is almost dizzying.

"Is there anything in there about Kamloops?" said Pad. "That's where I saw kids and mothers scratching around in the trash for something to eat."

*I passed a deserted Indian village in Kamloops. On either
side of the one wide, dusty street were warped wooden
huts. There was not a soul on the street. At the far end of
the street was a line of washed rags tied to a hut from the
only tree. Tied to that tree was an old Indian saddle-horse.
Two or three chickens were clucking about in the dryness
of the dusty back yard of the seemingly one inhabited
house of that village. Otherwise all was desolate.*

*In Kamloops there are more Indians than whites. What
whites there are, are either prospectors or tramps. Every
time I meet an Indian, he greets me with a "How," and I
say, "O.K. Joe." Despite their poorness, they are hospitable
and peaceful.*

At Prince Rupert Joe traded work for a room at the "headquarters
for all mining men, tourists, and commercial travelers." In the hotel
some characters caught his cartoonist's eye.

*The proprietress, Mrs. Black, must be one of those eccentric
millionairesses. She is over seventy, drinks like a hellion,
and works in the kitchen from 5:30 in the morning to 8
at night. She has a crabby-looking face, although that
belies her true character, which, I think, deep down is
kindness and considerateness toward all who do right by
her. She owns the post office and from what I've heard,
almost half the buildings in town.*

*Then there is Doris. There was insanity in her family
and she shows it. She wears a wild array of blond hair
above her big, blue, sharp eyes. She has fourteen or fifteen
cats and kittens all over the house. She also has a hen
house, a pond of ducks, two goats and four rabbits. These*

are her pets. Whenever she has a few minutes off, she whispers sweet nothings into the kittens' ears. She stands by with her hands folded in front of her and her head cocked to one side when she sees the momma cat carrying the young meandering kitten by the back of its neck back to their nest under the furnace. She has such a motherly look in her eyes. Yesterday I was in the basement and she comes tearing down the stairs with a hen in one arm and a red-haired kitten in the other. Mrs. Black had just kicked her out of the kitchen.

Old George, the bartender, is a long, slim, red-faced *guy. He is the most sober-looking gentleman I've ever seen. He is so cold and business-like in his every move. I was in the saloon and watched him for a few moments skim the foam off the beer in his icy, precise manner.*

For a tramp, though, things were looking grim.

It has been cold and rainy every day. At night I cover myself with a heavy quilt.

I walked around town today. It is deader than a Sunday in Philadelphia. Hanging on a telegraph pole were a few black bear skins. I looked in a window and saw some totem poles and a letter opener made of bone. Then it started to rain and I went back to my room.

It's only about a hundred miles to Ketchikan, Alaska, but I don't know how I'll ever make it. I'm not going to walk because the roads are flooded; there are not trains running there and I can't get on a boat, so I guess I'll have to be the fox and the sour grapes.

As a last resort he was considering stowing away on a ship when...

...there was a break in the weather and I was all ready to start east, when I was chased by a railroad detective. He asked me where I was from. No sooner had I opened my mouth than he had caught my American accent, which was that darned lazy southern drawl I had acquired I don't know where.

Those Stepin Fetchit films, no doubt.

Joe became a houseguest of the Canadian border police. The American Consul in Prince Rupert wired Sonny's family for ten dollars to spring him. They sent it. The consul wrote Pop Teller that Sonny was free and on his way.

He left for Ketchikan, Alaska, last evening on an American halibut schooner. He was in good health and as the salmon-canning season is under way in Alaska I have every reason to believe he will secure employment. He was strongly urged to write to you.

Respectfully yours,
G. C. Woodward
American Consul

Pop Teller promptly replied:

Dear Sir,
Permit me to thank you most heartily for the kindness and consideration you have shown my boy during his stay in Prince Rupert, also for helping him aboard the halibut

*schooner which will take him, let us hope safely, to
Alaska.*

*I feel that you have done in this peculiar case vastly more
than your official duty calls for; in fact there is a touch of
that fine humanitarian spirit, as exemplified in your helping a strange boy among strangers, that I believe that if
there were more men of broadmindedness and breadth of
character as you have evinced in this particular instance,
this world would be a much better place to live in, and boys
would not be obliged to go to Alaska for a job.*

*Thanking you again for your kindness toward my boy,
I beg to remain, Sir, very gratefully and respectfully,*

Joseph Teller, Sr.

IX

As a precaution against seasickness, Joe, the first-time sailor, fasted for
nine hours before the trip out of Prince Rupert. The boat left at 3 A.M.
He arrived in Ketchikan at 3 P.M. July 12, 1933, and went straight to the
post office.

*Dear Yap,
So arrives gradually de dope from his first ocean voyage.
At 8 knots per hour in a 32-foot fishing boat named
Thor it took exactly 12 hours from Prince Rupert to
Ketchikan. My only companions were the skipper and the
boatswain, both Swedes. As I stand here, I can still feel
the boat rocking under my feet...*

By the next day the romance of fish-canning had palled a bit.

Dear Works [his family, as in "the whole works"]
I spent some time among the canneries today. I sat down
on some planking and watched the beheading of a boat-
load of 40 to 60 lb. halibut. Half the town is built on pil-
ing and planks. The other half is on the side of a hill.
Here and there is a totem pole. In conclusion all I can say
is you shouldn't smell from herring.

Dear Yap,
Between Eskimos, Indians, and Pekingese, I'm going
crazy. I was around the fish today, halibut, salmon, wit
stinking ones. Tanks god can't find job in canneries! Tour
boat came in today. Heh, heh, look, a tourist. Stands there
with a stack of picture cards. "Very educational," she says,
and looks at me.

"It rained all the time," said Pad. "The only time there was any life
in town was when somebody like Douglas Fairbanks would come in on
his yacht. That was good for a day or so of excitement."

I'm still here and I can neither get out nor get out. After
bothering all the hotel and shopkeepers in town, I went
down to the docks and bothered all the skippers to take me
to some other port, all to no avail.
I talked with an old fisherman. He was telling me
stories and I was lounging on a gangplank, listening to
all his narrations, and trying to seem as interested as
possible.

He told Yappy how he snoozed his way into a job.

*Last night I fell asleep in the lobby of the Gilmore Hotel.
They kicked me out about 12. I went across the street,
bummed some coffee, and went to the Stedman Hotel,
where they put me up for the night. In the morning the
boss began pounding on my door, hollering to beat hell. So
I says, all right, wait a minute. He was all flusticated
because he could not find my name in the register. I
explain and, damn it, he gives me a job!*

X

He approached his new work as the Stedman Hotel's odd-job man
philosophically.

*I spent a rather enjoyable few minutes in the bar-room this
afternoon shellacking the horns of a caribou. I also
cleaned its eyes and brushed its mane. Then I painted the
baseboard a shining black to match the black marble
trimmings of the mirrors. We fastened the head on the
middle of the wall above the mirrors and bar.*

*The head, alone, was mounted twenty years ago. It was
shot in the mountains close by (I never knew the beast
had mountains.)*

*Although when I brushed it with the broom, a few
hairs came out, still it is quite handsome. The front of its
mane is like the beard of a goat. Its glazed eyes hold an
expression of boldness, proudness, timidness, and vicious-
ness, while its fur is viscous with the grease and grit of a
century. When I brushed it, the viscosity was converted
into an oily sheen.*

While I was working, a crowd of trappers, prospectors, and what-nots gathered about. From them I soon overheard all that one could possibly know of the history and ways of caribous. Now there is a law against killing them.

I've seen these caribou qualities and expressions on several human beings, yet never have I seen nor care to see the head of one of them fastened to the wall over the mantel in our parlor.

"The bar had a brass trough on the front of it, so that the patrons could pee without having to leave the bar," added Pad.

He became the resident house painter.

I finished painting the new toilet yesterday. I gave it two coats of gray enamel and one heavy one on the cement floor. All the boys are saying it is the spiffiest toilet in town.

To-day, as I will do on all fair days henceforward, I was painting on the outside. If they expect me to finish that outside job, I will be here for at least two years—the place is so big and the fair days are so few and far between. On other days I paint the rooms that need it. So you see that when I leave here, if I am not a first class painter, Rembrandt was a gandy dancer.

A "gandy dancer" was a railroad laborer.

"That's about the time I started going bald," mused Pad serenely. "I wouldn't be at all surprised if there was something funny in all that white lead paint..."

Joe's pay was four dollars a day. Thirty-six dollars for nine days' work. Not bad for a kid in Depression times. But there *were* a few minor expenses taken out...

> 2 meal tickets—$10.00
> Room—$8.00 (to August 1)
> 2 meal tickets—$10.00

Which left a total of eight dollars cash, or eighty-nine cents a day. But, as he wrote the family,

> *Harder the work, so the lesser the pay.*
> *Thus philosophically, hard work is play.*

His boss shared his attitude.

> *I've given the boss several reasons for firing me, but it just doesn't seem to click with him. Last week one afternoon we had a little sunshine. He told me to get out on the roof and tar the skylights.*
>
> *Well, I got out on the roof and sat down with my back against a sunny side of the upper story, faced the mountains and water, got out my pen-knife and began whittling away on the handle of my putty-knife. Soon I fell to dreaming and anon to slumber.*
>
> *Then I heard as if far away, "Joe, O Joe!" The boss had come up for me to help him move something downstairs. I just sat there. He hollered some more. So I yelled back, "Yo!" Then he came around and saw me basking in the sunlight.*
>
> *A big smile came upon his face as he saw me sprawling there. "Well," he said, as he came over, "I don't blame*

you." He sat down beside me and started telling me about the pleasant moments in his life. He was smiling nicely all the while and, as I was a good listener, continued shooting the bull for about half an hour. Then he arose and stretched and said lazily, "Aw, I gotta go to work now, but you can stay here if you want to." So I stayed there and he went to work.

XI

Dear Yap,
Being, as it was, quite a time since I've received mail from anybody, I was determined to get some meaning out of yours. So right away I see a word—"lrrufwe." I say, what the hell and run downstairs for a dictionary. But there's no such word there. Then I see—"asley." But this time my searching was rewarded, for where "asley" should be I found "asleep." Thus for two hours I worked in my endeavor to distinguish what should be from what might have been. And thus your prophecy of it taking all my spare time and most of my patience was entirely fulfilled.

Yappy bragged of a sexual encounter, and Joe reminded him of the hazards Yap had risked:

So, a perverted gigolo you became. Noo, dope! You need maybe clopps, syph-amonia, plurosy, high-balls, or something another time. It's not enough you run around with a busted toe?

Joe wrote his family about Ketchikan's oddballs.

> *There is a certain Chinaman named Charlie. Of him*
> *there is a sad, sad story. Four years ago he was dejected*
> *and disgracefully sent to roam the streets. He had dis-*
> *closed the secrets of his tong and the punishment of this*
> *was everlasting grief reigned by his own superstitious*
> *brain. He lags around in a single terribly ragged overcoat.*
> *His trousers cling tightly above his ankles. Out of his*
> *stretched, soleless shoes stick dirty white socks with spots*
> *of brown where his flesh shows through. On his head is*
> *an ancient cap which has been pulled down so often that*
> *if it wasn't for his unshorn locks, which are black and*
> *are already creeping over the collar of his coat, it would*
> *be resting peacefully on his snubby nose. His beardless*
> *face is a calm brown. He would indeed make a sorry*
> *sight if hair grew on his chin, for he dare not cut it. There*
> *is a mixture of bewilderment and reverie in his brown*
> *eyes constantly.*
>
> *He is short and skinny and, I'd say, about twenty-eight*
> *years old.*
>
> *He refuses money and clothing. I know not if he eats,*
> *or where he gets it, if he does. He dares not hang himself*
> *for fear his soul would come out the wrong place. He's*
> *sure in a hellofafix.*

Joe's sisters asked for a snapshot in his best Sunday go-to-church clothes.

> *I believe that phrase would be more appropriate as Go-To-*
> *Hell clothes. In dress, I hope to remain plain Sonny:*

clumsy shoes,—dark, creaseless, shining trousers,—
unpressed, open-necked shirt,—heavy white sox,—and an
old dark-gray sweater. These I hold dearly and very close
to me.

My evenings are usually occupied in my quiet, little
room. In fact I remain awake until eleven or twelve
almost every night, even tho' the ten bells of the church
denote the bedtime of all good people. What do I do?
Seemingly nothing. I merely sit with my teeth in my
mouth, as it were.

His family's constant hunger for news elicited a reply—in verse:

I wring my hands,
  I twist my face;
Harsh reprimands
  Await my case
If there's no word from Sonny.

My eyes must gleam;
  My brain must work;
I need some scheme;
  I'll be alert
So they'll get word from Sonny.

I'll find some way,
  Something to write;
I'll think all day
  And write tonight;
They must have word from Sonny.

Sometimes in the dead of night a Muse came to inspire that "word from Sonny."

Last night about one o'clock, I was suddenly aroused by
the unfamiliar sound of silence. The rain had ceased.
Everything was calm, save the wheezing snore of the man
bound in assuredly not heavenly dreams coming from the
next room. I hastily dressed and soon was mingling with
the gentle breezes along the waterfront.
  The heavens were overcast with black satin bellies
tinged with dull silver. It seemed like so many aristocratic

*ladies gloating o'er their domain, ready at any moment to
belch forth great gusts of rain as their united moods dictate.*

*In this grand ballroom of darkness, these queenly indi-
viduals collide with one another. They become frightened in
the blackness. They scream and draw forth pins from their
garments and hair, and commence pricking one another.*

*Soon they are all in horrible combat. They roar in rage
and pain. Small drops of glistening blood ooze from their
many tiny wounds.*

*In a little while they become so weak that there are but
hoarse groans. Even this ceases. They are unconscious, but
now their lives are dripping away in one continual down-
fall of drops. Their satin robes, covered with the ooze of
their bloated bellies, incarnadine.*

They are dead and their reign is over.

But, alas, their rain was not over. Joe spent the endless watery,
overcast days watching Ketchikan's citizens perilously negotiating the
soggy wooden sidewalks. Joe painted this in a sonnet for his family.

> *Up here where women swagger and men sway,*
> *To hold, not lose their equilibrium —*
> *On slippery planks of this aquarium*
> *Where human beings dwell from day to day; —*
> *The best of weather here, if I may say,*
> *Is unfit for a sanitarium...*
> *As dog-meat for a vegetarian.*
> *Or snow in Georgia in the month of May...*

As I read this aloud at the kitchen table, Pad closed his eyes and
finished the rest of his poem from memory.

Yet in this godforsaken town so drear,
The people are so seemingly content,
    And when, mayhaps, the weather should be clear,
They just remain, as ever, continent.
    For soon, they know, another cloud will burst—
    And thus, they, unconcernedly, are cursed.

"Is this your father's influence?" asked Mam. "Or did you learn about poetry in school?"

"Nah, you can't blame it on any one person."

XII

The young vegetarian of limited means wrote with special gusto about food.

Yesterday I struck upon an economy plan. Being as I've been paying about seventy or seventy-five cents for each meal, I decided to do a little meal-preparing on my own.

So I went to a Piggly-Wiggly Store where things are cheaper. This is what I bought and the price of each article: one loaf of cracked-whole-wheat bread—twenty cents; a quarter pound of butter—fifteen cents; a quarter pound of pineapple cream cheese—twenty-five cents; a quart of milk—twenty-five cents with a nickel deposit for the bottle; a pound of dates—twenty cents; a half-pound of shelled walnuts—thirty cents; a box of Wheaties—twenty cents; a head of lettuce—25 cents; a pound of tomatoes— 30 cents; a head of cabbage—15 cents; a bunch of carrots—89 cents; two apples—ten cents; 3 oranges—15 cents. Well, from all these I managed to make three substantial

meals. And I still have a few leaves of cabbage and some dates.

I made some of those fruit and nut sandwiches that we used to eat on Saturday afternoons and Sundays on the boat on the river. I happened to glance in the mirror and I couldn't withhold a silly grin. My both cheeks were full with all my mouth could hold and my eyes were sparkling with the delicious sensation.

As for being an economy plan, well, I saved about a nickel anyway.

The sandwiches had their effect.

*Poor little me. 192 pounds. Damn those sandwiches.
Every one tastes better than the last. Each one is
approximately an inch and a half thick. And I eat three
or four every time I sit down. No wonder my brain is
sluggish.*

Alas, an obstacle to gluttony:

*This isn't an inspiration; it's merely the urge of my new
wisdom tooth. For the last few days the gum way back in
my mouth was troubling me. Today a new tooth sprouted
forth. I could hardly open my mouth but for half an
inch.*

*But, oh, the misery of it all. You know those sand-
wiches I was telling you about? Well, I had to sit on them
for a few minutes so that they would become thin enough
to squeeze between my teeth. Isn't that discouraging?*

There's even a whiff of his fruit sandwiches in his parody of William
Blake's style.

*Pretty apple, where growest thou?
I grow upon a spreading bough.
    Shining apple, how growest thou?
I grow like any man or cow.
    Smiling apple, when growest thou?
I grow by sun that gods endow.
    Apple of wisdom, why growest thou?
I grow for nuts like you to chow.*

[81]

In time, he expanded his culinary repertoire.

> *I've taken to batchin', as they call it. I've got the cutest lit-*
> *tle green single-burner electric stove and a little kettle*
> *with a green handle to match, and the darlingest cup and*
> *saucer, and a silver-plated knife and fork and soup-spoon*
> *and teaspoon. Goodness gracious, I feel like a brand new*
> *bride.*
>
> *For my supper, which I have all evening to prepare, I*
> *make one of my famous vegetable soups. Already I've*
> *added a new flavor to that old-fashioned soup. I melt in a*
> *hunk of Swiss cheese. Boy, maybe it's not delicious! I*
> *supplement my evening repast with hot water and milk*
> *and graham crackers.*

Pad at the kitchen table dipped his unbuttered, extra-crispy toast into his soothing "cambric tea" (hot water, slightly cooled with milk) and smiled. "Every night before I go to bed I still have my hot-water-and-milk."

XIII

In October the family wrote him that they were moving to a new house. Just to torment Clayton, Joe hinted about a hidden treasure.

> *I hope the old house is still empty when I get back,*
> *because I've a few things of personal importance hidden*
> *behind several of the bricks in the cellar. But don't let that*
> *worry you. Because when Clayton helped you move, you*
> *know his old eagle eye doesn't miss a thing...*

Clayton bit. He smelled cash.

> *If you think it will not overtax your mentality to the*
> *breaking point, then please hesitate long enough to*
> *attempt to recall what it was that you hid, if anything,*
> *and where, if anywhere. I shall never forget the light of joy*
> *that suffused your Father's features when he read of*
> *unearthing any filthy lucre that you might have hidden.*
> *Now, any child who either consciously or unwittingly*
> *causes their parents' nerves to falsely tingle is certainly not*
> *displaying filial devotion and respect.*

Joe ignored the question, instead announcing how he planned to blow the Ketchikan wages he had saved with his "economy plan."

> *I've come to the conclusion that the only thing fit to live*
> *up in this country is a totem pole. When I needs must*
> *abandon my evening strolls for fear of being smacked on*
> *the head by a hunk of hail, that's going a little too far.*
> *So four days from now I'll be going south like a big*
> *shot. Yes, sir, boy, I've made my mind up that I'm going to*
> *travel First Class on the biggest boat that visits*
> *Ketchikan: the S.S. Alaska, from New York, sailing south*
> *on Saturday, October 28, 1933, at 1 P.M.*

Once aboard, he wrote two versions of the First Class experience. The first was to his family.

> *Dear Pop and Works,*
> *It would do your heart good to see these lusty, rough,*
> *weather-beaten Alaskans sitting in a first class dining*

salon trying to keep their awkward appearance in compliance with the unwritten laws of table manners. These who have spent most of their lives in cabins, prospecting or fishing, are now going south, probably to visit friends or blow their hard-earned summer stakes in a big city.

They have their own ideas of what the well-dressed man will wear at dinner. A light gray suit, a black flannel shirt, and a red necktie constitute their apparel. And of course a shot of liquor to sort of brace their nerves at the table seems to affect them wonderfully.

You should see their big horny hands as they attempt daintily (that is, hook their little finger) the process of conveying the food from dish to mouth.

The ungraceful erectness of a desire to act correctly is most becoming, or rather amusing, to my eye.

Once in a while they become sobered and at once extremely nervous and impatient. Can you blame them? It's enough to sober anybody. You get your soup and about twenty minutes after you're through, they bring around the next course. Well, I don't eat soup and I had to wait about a half hour before they brought my lettuce, beets, and cheese.

Anyway, when these swarthy mugs become sobered, they look around to see if anyone is looking. Then they reach for their inside coat pocket and sorta try to push their face in it. They shake their head once or twice, swallow, and the frightened appearance is replaced with a smile. It seems they carry straws around in their bottles.

The second version, the one he sent to Yappy, was a little less highfalutin.

Dear Yap,

*Imagine me sitting in a dining salon among these big shot
tourists. Imagine having some mug dressed in white shov-
ing the chair under you before you sit at the table. Imagine
a guy asking you how many lumps of sugar you should
like in your coffee and pouring the cream in for you. And
calling you "sir"—GRRR.—*

*And holding the menu card for you and you got to
choose from a whole bunch of fancy crap. So I just says,—
gimme some vegetables—he says—we've a splendid fu-lay
min-you or somp'n—I says: Nuts! jeesus crist!—it seems
everybody in the room heard me and the waiter seemed so
shocked. Anyhow I slip a two bit hunk for that damn
punk under my plate every shot.*

*And everybody running around on deck with a
bearskin coat or somp'n and me open necked.*

*Well, boy, I hope that's a lesson for me never to ride as
a first class passenger again.*

Aw Nuts
Me

XIV

After three and a half months of rain and fish, Sonny headed straight
for California to bask in the sun.

*Shcrumpfl. Sunday afternoon and I'm sprawling beneath
a walnut tree. For the last hour, I haven't moved and have
been eating walnuts almost continually. You see, I have no
reason to move as all about me they have fallen and there
are so many. There are some rows of tomatoes, red,*

luscious ones, behind me, and across the highway are
golden yellow pears, and down the road about a dozen
black fig trees. What a vegetarian's paradise!
    Everything's in harvest and ready to be picked. But this
dear child thinks he needs a vacation, and, having noth-
ing to hinder that thought, I'm merely taking one.

So, till my swinish nature has departed,
I guess I'll have to finish what I started.

Yappy in reply didn't make Philadelphia in November sound very
appealing.

Back here the monotony is unequalled in the annals of my
long career of corner-lounging. The streets seem to have
taken on a perpetual coating of filth, paper, herring,
decayed vegetation, etc., and plenty of falling leaves. In
short she is one no good city.

All is dull. All is drab
When everything is bare.
With disposition of the crab
I've taken to pulling my hair.

Joe was doing odd jobs in California and still meeting people who
behaved like cartoons.

I mowed the lawn of a Communist today, who kept
chasing me around the lawn waving his hands and
preaching.

"It's nothing without the cufflinks."

He was still capturing the essence of a situation in a few lines:

> *I was resting in a vacant lot in the residential district of*
> *Chula Vista, when a five or six year old boy came over*
> *and asked me, "Are you a tramp?"*
> *I said, "What do you think?"*
> *Then he asked, "Where is your wife?"*
> *"I have no wife."*
> *"Why don't you get one?"*
> *"I can't afford to keep one."*
> *Finally he spun around on one foot and suggested very*
> *seriously, "Why don't you go to the dog-pound?"*

Joe picked up his mail in San Diego. Clayton had fallen for the story about the treasure in the cellar.

> *I was sitting on the steps of the San Diego post office*
> *reading my mail when I came to that part in Clayton's*
> *letter where he was down in the old cellar looking for that*
> *loose brick in the wall where I hid my filthy lucre. At the*
> *time I was eating an orange. The juice came out of my*
> *nose and with laughing and orange juice, my clean white*
> *shirt was all splattered up.*
> *I'm still rather groggy from the sudden change of a*
> *dreary rain to bright sunshine. I'm in the best of health,*
> *brown as a nut, but my brain is soggy.*

So soggy that even California's railroad police could scarcely get his attention, as he told Yappy.

Flopped in a box-car. A couple of bulls came around and whistled at me and hollered and finally took to throwing sticks at me before they managed to awaken me. Got fingerprinted and kicked out of San Diego.

Well, get your tin horns ready, keed. I'll be home for el año nuevo if nothing happens.

In late November Joe wrote his family that he was coming home. Joe, Sr., responded:

My dear Boy:
Your letters have always been a source of joy and entertainment to all of us. Some of your letters have even the merit of a literary, poetical, as well as highly frolicsome and amusing touch to them.

That letter wherein you describe your own method of preparing and cooking a beet soup was truly a masterpiece in its line. You would be surprised, if you knew how many people outside ourselves have read your description of a culinary process. This is just one sample to show you what I mean.

In fact, all your letters, with few exceptions, meant to us many moments of untold pleasure and delight. But like all writings, from the most celebrated authors and poets to the humblest tyro, there is to be found this fact—that it is the single verse, a single passage, or just one line that often sends a thrill through the reader's heart and soul, that even a great lyric or epic poem will never accomplish. The letter wherein you told us that you are on your way home is what I mean. "I'm coming home!" Just three simple words. But how significant they are to those to whom they are addressed!

The joy and festival spirit that permeated our domestic atmosphere is beyond my power to describe. The most I can do is to say, with Tennyson, "I would my tongue could utter the thoughts that arise in me."

With sincere wishes for your well-being and happiness.

Pop

J. T.

Clayton, too, was happy Joe was coming home. He desperately wanted company (and, of course, a little money) for his next adventure.

Please come on home immediately and we will try to scrape a few bucks together so that we can leave for the tropics very soon. I will finish my stories and hope to god we win this time. I think we make a good team; what do you say?

He offered to "shoot out and meet" Joe in Washington, D.C., on his way home. But Joe was still a long way from Washington.

One of these here Texas-raised so and sos gave me a wrong steer. He points out, he says, "This train right here is going to San Antonio." So I got on that train and now I'm in Kansas City, Kansas. Heart-rending, ain't it?

On December 8, 1933, Joe wrote from Pensacola, Florida, on a postcard to Yappy,

Well, I think I got all the states I missed down in this
neck of the woods—although I had no intention of getting
them.

Clayton's plan to meet Joe in Washington evaporated. On December 12, 1933, in Washington, Joe wrote,

No Clayton,
No Waitin'.

That was the last card Joe sent from his trip. Two days later he was home. His farewell to the road was one wry couplet, which I discovered in an otherwise unused leather-bound diary near the bottom of the hobo shoebox:

So somewhere in the Keeper's book you'll see
Beside my name, "Ten days for Vagrancy."

"I just adore love stories."

A Streetcar Named Desire

I

Joe was home but all his corner-lounging cronies were gone. Leapy had gone abroad as an Ordinary Seaman. Shooie and Joe's other chums (except Clayton, of course) had jobs. Yappy had gone out on the road, and Joe kept in touch with letters with little drawings in them. But Yappy sure didn't make a return to tramping sound romantic.

> *The road is washed up! Transient camps over the entire country—railroads are trying to diminish the unwanted riders—people are wise to a guy on the road. And boy, in some places you have to hustle to get by.*
>
> *Stand in line at a transient camp—the youngsters just starting out, thinking they are doing something; the old timers growling and <u>crabby</u>! Who wouldn't be crabby if one waked up to the realization of a lazy, feckless, parasitical, wasted life, and what a life compared to what he <u>"might have done."</u>*
>
> *How are you coming along? I showed some of your cartoons to a few guys and boy did they laugh.*

Joe turned twenty-one. Time to grow up.

II

I went for a walk after dinner and returned with a bunch of sunflowers from a street vendor. "These would make a good still life," I said.

"Then you paint it," said Pad. "I'll teach you."

Pad set up the easel and canvas in the studio, while I looked over the still-life props on the high shelf that clings perilously to the plaster wall over the bench on which Pad keeps his sketch pads and tubes of paint. I picked out a white pitcher and started to put the sunflowers in it.

"I'd stay away from white," said Pad. "White is hard to paint."

I put away the white pitcher and picked out a red terra-cotta vase from Mexico.

"That's good. It goes nice. See, you're learning."

"How did you learn to paint?" I asked.

"I went to school for it. After I got home from my peregrinations," he said, savoring the word, "my father said to me, 'So, Sonny, what are you going to do for a living?'

"I thought about how much I liked mechanical drawing and said, 'I could draw.'

"Pop believed in the power of the printed word. He found me an art course from the International Correspondence School in Scranton, Pennsylvania. It was real good. I still have the books. Now, open up that closet and pick a backdrop. There's a million colors in there."

I picked out a piece of deep purple velvet. Pad slipped into the storeroom. I hung the velvet from the batten on the wall behind the still-life table.

Pad came back with a dozen old drawings of assorted sizes in charcoal and ink. He handed them to me. They were some of his class assignments from the International Correspondence School.

While I looked at them, he inspected my backdrop. "Attaboy," he said. "That purple's good with the yeller of the flowers. And it's dark,

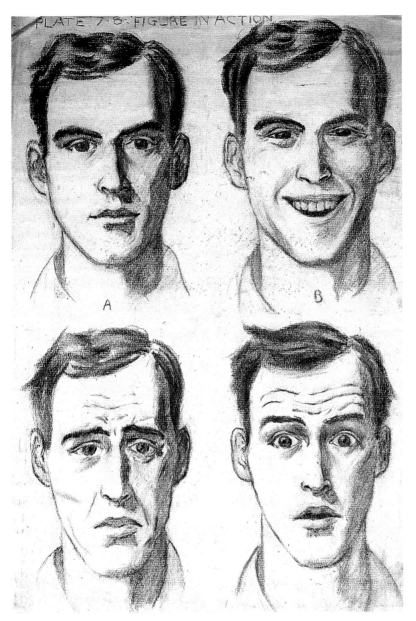

The handiest model was in the mirror.

too. So you have a dark, a medium—that's the pot—and a light—that's the flowers."

The correspondence school drawings were dated from 1934 to 1937, and they all had formal titles: "Light and Shade," "Figure in Action," and so forth. Each was graded "A" in red pencil.

I held up one, a satirical newspaper spread about Hitler. "We thought he was a big joke in those days," Pad shrugged.

Self-portrait, 1939, 12" × 16", Irene Teller   *Self-portrait, 1939, 12" × 16", Joe Teller*

Spring Garden Street Kitchen Table, 1939, 20" × 16", Joe Teller

Proud Pitcher, 1959, 12" x 16", Joe Teller

Wild Flowers, 1962, 16" x 20", Joe Teller

Bowl and Pitcher, 1968, 24" x 18", Joe Teller

Menagerie, 1974, 20" × 31", Joe Teller

Happy Thanksgiving, 1979, 18" × 24", Joe Teller

Slam Dunk,
1981, 28" × 24", Joe Teller

Spitfire, 1985, 28" × 20", Joe Teller

Landscape, 1987, 42" × 30", Joe Teller

Vegas, 1993, 24" × 20", Joe Teller

Rosey's Bar, 1999, 16" × 20", Irene Teller

My Little Jewel, 1999, 8" × 10", Joe Teller

Self-portraits, clockwise from top left, 1977, 8" × 9"; 1988, 12" × 18"; 1994, 18" × 24"; 1998, 18" × 24", Joe Teller

Self-portrait Chewing Tobacco, 1969, 18" x 24", finger painting in oil on canvas, Joe Teller

The Russian Lovers, 1998, 24" × 30", Joe Teller

He handed me a stick of charcoal and I started drawing. I drew big, fat sunflowers filling the canvas.

"Now, hold your horses," he said. "First thing, you have to draw in the line of the table. That's important."

I sighed and reached for a yardstick.

"What the hell are you doing?" he said.

"The edge of the table is a straight line."

"Put that away and draw with your eye. In art when a line *looks* straight, it *is* straight."

"Okay," I said, "but I'd really rather not have the edge of the table in the picture, because then I'll have to show the vase and then it'll look like I'm ripping off van Gogh."

"Don't worry," he said. "It *won't* look like van Gogh."

I was smearing the purple oil paint on the canvas very carefully with a flexible steel painting knife. It seemed perverse to lay in the background before painting the vase or the flowers. But that's what Pad had said to do and that's what I was doing. He was dozing in his chair.

When he opened his eyes, I was just cleaning the last of the purple off the knife.

"It cost fifteen dollars a month," he said.

"What did?"

"Correspondence school. Sometimes my father paid and sometimes I earned the money. I was a blacksmith's assistant where they fixed cart wheels and shoed horses. Then my father made friends with one of his streetcar passengers who ran a coal yard, and he gave me a job unloading train cars—with a shovel. My nose got all stuffed up doing that.

"Then my sister Eva—she worked at the *Inquirer,* so she always knew everything—heard about a free art school, the first one in the country. It was called the Graphic Sketch Club. A big textile guy—what the hell was his name? He converted a south Philadelphia church into an art

PLATE 7-8: PENCIL, CHARCOAL, AND CRAYON

Eva: sister, editor's assistant, opera lover.

museum; then he bought the house next door and turned that into studios for classes.

"Eva said he had the best teachers in Philadelphia down there, and he paid them good money, too. What the hell, it was gonna be free for me! So during the day I'd do my little part-time jobs and work on the correspondence course, then from seven to nine at night I went down to Graphic."

"What do I do now?"

"Go ahead and put in the vase and flowers. And don't be so damn niggly. You won't know what you have until there's no more white canvas showing through. Get it all covered. Then you can start to think. I've had enough for one night. I'm going downstairs. Have fun, goddamit!"

Okay, I thought. I *would* have fun. I squeezed a tube and out came a four-inch squirt of cadmium orange. I took a big, fat knife and began to paint.

When you're painting, nothing exists but the picture. Time stops. When I finished my sunflowers, I was amazed to find it was past eleven o'clock. I wiped my hands with turpentine and rags and went downstairs.

"Well, I've just finished my first oil painting," I declared.

"And you had fun, didn't you!" beamed Mam.

"I had a grand time." I lathered up my hands with soap in the kitchen sink. "Where's Pad?"

"He's gone up. The blood pressure pill knocks him right out."

Mam tapped a finger on the address label of a copy of *TV Guide* lying on the kitchen table. "Look at this. The subscription doesn't run out for another six years. We'll still be getting it long after we're dead."

III

As the sun set on a crisp fall evening in 1936, a slim, twenty-eight-year-old woman with a sharply cut profile, large brown eyes, and dark curly hair rode the streetcar.

Irene had finished her lunchtime job at the steam table at the tony Colonnade cafeteria in the underground arcade in the old Bankers Trust building. She had traveled five miles north and dutifully dined at home with her parents and fifteen-year-old brother. And now she was traveling south again, another five miles toward the Graphic Sketch Club.

"And—eh—I might have some spinach—oh—eh—if you tell me how you cook it."

To Irene, Philadelphia seemed as dark and cramped as a rat hole. She had lived on a farm for ten years and only recently moved to the city. She missed her friends. She missed the animals. And most of all she missed the light, streaming in the windows on all sides of the farmhouse. Her family's brick row house seemed like a crypt.

A little after seven P.M. she got off the streetcar at Seventh and Catherine streets and crossed to the stern Romanesque church. Though it was dark, she wasn't afraid. A man had chased her on the subway one night, but she had outrun him, then whirled around and socked him in the face. Raised on a farm, you learn to handle animals.

Before tonight she had never had an art lesson. When she was a child, her Aunt Belle had given her crayons and praised her drawings. In any free moment she sat by herself and used a fountain pen to copy the photographs out of the newspapers. She had decided she would grow up to be an art teacher.

There were no identifying signs on the outside of the building. Bright light glowed seductively in the windows on the upper floors of the adjoining brick building. She walked up the front steps and under the arch of the entrance.

In each of the studios of the Graphic Sketch Club a dozen or so students sat on wooden chairs and painted or drew while instructors circulated to critique.

On the ground floor was a small art supply store.

"I bought a pad and pencil. I went into the room where they were drawing casts of Greek sculptures. I sat down and started to draw a mask.

"The instructor walked up to me and said, 'I think this would work better if you didn't make it so large.'

"I said, 'It's the first time I ever drew something like this.'

"'Well,' he said, 'this is the best first drawing I ever saw.'"

.   .   .

"To this day I don't know how my father found out about the Graphic Sketch Club or why he ever told me about it. My father had no use for artists," said Mam. "He was a fiend for money. It was only natural. He grew up dirt poor in Delaware and had to support his mother and sister. When he was ten he walked into a department store and told the manager they needed somebody to hold the door open for customers, and they gave him a job. He could get money out of anybody."

Mam laid out a tissue on the kitchen table to catch crumbs. Then she took out a single slice of bread and spread peanut butter on it.

"Dad used to brag about how he cheated people. And when I was little, we were always moving, always running away from somebody. I think now he must have been a bootlegger."

She folded her bread in half and took a dainty bite of her sandwich. "But eventually he had enough saved up to buy his farm. Forty-eight acres in County Line, Pennsylvania, no less, where rich people had fox hunts. Now he was happy. He got up every morning at four-thirty to milk the cows and feed hot oatmeal to the hogs. Then he took a train into Philadelphia to his day job at the Keystone Telephone Company. He had a big corner office. He didn't have to cheat people any more. Have some peanut butter."

"No thanks, it gives me nightmares."

She reflected. "Mother hated the country. She was an elegant woman from the city and there she was in a farmhouse all alone. She used to say, 'I'm making cupcakes today and if you stay home from school and help me, you can lick the pan.' Mother and I raised a runt pig as a pet. My father slaughtered it. He just thought a pig was food. Neither Mother nor I ate any meat that winter."

She wiped the corners of her mouth with another tissue.

"But I loved the farm. At last I was in one place for ten whole years, where I could go to school one grade after the other instead of my education being cut up like a jigsaw puzzle."

"But at least you'd learned to read, right?"

She nodded. "Sheer perseverance," she said.

"Living in one place, I could finally have friends. Margaret lived on the next farm over."

Margaret has remained Mam's best friend for eighty years. She's a frank redhead fond of old Scotch whisky and diamond rings.

"We used to ride the horses. Oh, we must have been a sight. Pretty Irish Margaret on her dainty little pony, and tough, dark ol' Irene on her huge ol' Boy.

"That was the horse's name," she said, a little embarrassed. "He had been an army workhorse but they had to retire him because he would go crazy over any loud noise. Too many cannons, I guess. I think he was a special breed for cold weather. In the winter he'd grow coarse hair an inch thick all over his body and I would brush him..."

There's a certain smile that comes over Mam's face when she talks about horses. Her normally tight lips part and she shows her less-than-Hollywood-perfect teeth without fear of the camera. I've seen this same enchanted smile when she's painting a still life; watching the pink buds burst open on the lone hollyhock tree in the bricked backyard; eating a salad Pad has made. It's as if she is looking Life straight in its big brown horse's eyes, stroking its warm, sleek-coated jaw, and memorizing every individual hair, so that no detail will slip away unfeasted upon.

I suspect that Mam's ability to be shamelessly and helplessly abducted by flashes of beauty is what has always drawn Pad to her. And when Pad makes some daft joke that sets Mam laughing, she can't help but let loose with a beam of that rapture, aimed straight at him, an arrow right through the pacemaker.

IV

Suddenly I heard rapid footsteps descending lots of stairs and Pad burst into the kitchen. Mam looked up, frightened that Pad might be suffering fibrillation.

"You should see it, Irene! I got up to pee, so I thought I might as well look at the painting. Why the hell do I study this stuff all these years? It's wonderful, just wonderful. Irene, you better go see it before he goes and messes it up with refinements. I mean it. It's beautiful. No perspective, no shading. It's just *sunflowers* and they jump right out at you."

He pointed at me.

"He's a primitive. We've raised a goddamn primitive!"

V

Samuel S. Fleisher, the textile-millionaire founder of the Graphic Sketch Club, had invited "the world to come and learn art." Irene was attending two or three nights a week. Joe went every night, plunging into every medium with sinewy, ink-stained hands.

"I tried everything—etching, aquatints, sculpture. Sometimes I went six days a week, though Saturday was kids' day, so there were no nudies," said Pad.

"Everyone was so open and friendly," said Mam. "I remember one of the girls in Life Drawing class. She was a painter and then she'd model, too. She had such a nice figure and was as comfortable with her clothes off as you are with them on."

"And you met Pad in the Life class, right?"

"I must have talked to him now and then," said Mam. "I talked to everybody. I certainly didn't know him."

"You were the model monitor," said Pad. "At the beginning of a session, you would say, 'Pose, please.' Then at the end of twenty minutes, you would say, 'Rest.' The students could keep drawing, and the model could go have a smoke."

One night after class Irene got on the streetcar. It was empty. She took a seat by a window and opened the book she carried to keep her company on the way home.

Joe got on.

"She was the only one in the car," Pad said with a sly shrug. "And I was the only guy. So I sat down next to her."

"I was shocked. There were loads of empty seats. I thought it was very strange you sat right alongside me."

"We hit it off real good right from the beginning," said Pad. "It was the fickle finger of fate."

Irene began to go to the Graphic Sketch Club more often.

When one of the Graphic Sketchers suggested that a few congenial students form a small group to share the expense of a private *atelier* with their own models and still lifes (as he had heard the bohemian artists of Paris did), Joe and Irene joined.

The collective found a space on narrow Quince Street and named their group of eight or nine the Quince Group, imagining, no doubt, that in the future their biographers would allude to the influence of the Quince Group on the Philadelphia School of American Art. If what you're reading can be considered biography, well, then they were right.

On weeknights they worked at the studio. Every Saturday they went painting in the countryside.

"It was only one trolley ride away, but we found some wonderful painting places," grinned Mam. "When you have a stream running through woods—man!—you've got everything you need."

The Quince Group disbanded after less than a year, but Joe and Irene were going strong.

> MAM: *Eva played the mandolin, didn't she?*
> PAD: *Oh, yes. So nice. I played harmonica, but I could only play one piece on the piano. What was it?*
> MAM: *I don't recall.*
> PAD: *I played it for you a million times. It was…oh…*

KID: *A classical piece?*

PAD: *Yeah. Beethoven or something.*

KID: Moonlight Sonata?

PAD: *No. Maybe it was Wagner* [pronounced with an American *W* and a flat Philadelphian *a*].

KID: The Ride of the Valkyries?

PAD [rubbing his large hand across his bald head to squeeze out the information]: *No. Ahhhh. No—Is there a piece called the* William Tell Overture?

KID: *Sure* [sings].

PAD: *The Lone Ranger's theme song. That's it!*

When you love listening to your sweetheart play the *William Tell Overture* over and over again because it's the only tune he knows, you can be sure you're pretty far gone.

VI

Joe, being an artist, wasn't welcome in Irene's father's household.

"They didn't know me," said Pad. "I'd be seeing you home and saying goodnight and we'd be messing around in the vestibule and your mother would say 'Get out of here!'"

"That doesn't sound like my mother," Mam said. "She was always my defender. She was probably keeping you away from my father. He could be a very dangerous man," she added darkly.

Pad turned to me. "Never get married," he said, "unless you can't help it. And we couldn't. We were just too far in love or something. We just couldn't help it."

"What did your parents have to say when you told them?" I asked Mam.

"I don't recall talking about it with my parents," she said. "I must have told my mother. I just don't remember it."

"Would they have minded that Pad was Jewish?"

"I don't think they even knew what Jewish was," said Pad. "And *my* family was glad to get rid of me. When you get married you have to settle down. You can't be married and go bumming around."

"So we bought the marriage license for—how much was it, Joe?"

"Three dollars."

"And we set a date for the wedding. I didn't want a big to-do, but Joe's sisters pushed for it. Then they started to fight. Each one wouldn't come to the wedding if the others were there. That did it for me! So at eleven o'clock the night before we were supposed to be married, we got off the streetcar on Germantown Avenue and went up to the minister's house."

"What denomination?" I asked.

"Who knows?" said Pad. "He just had a card in the window: Ellsworth Erskine Jackson. Available for weddings, christenings, and funerals."

"We knocked on the door and told him what we wanted," Mam continued. "Well, he told us his wife would need to be the witness. For heaven's sake, what did we need a witness for?"

"And he called upstairs."

"She came down all dressed up," said Mam. "I guess she changed out of her pajamas."

"Then, just like that, he married us."

"And he read us a passage from Genesis," said Mam. "He called it 'Joseph, Teller of Dreams.' Imagine him thinking of that! In the middle of the night!"

"So we paid him for marrying us—how much was it?"

"Two dollars. And we each went off to our individual homes and didn't tell anyone what happened."

.   .   .

The next day Mr. and Mrs. Joe Teller picked up Irene's furniture from her parents' house and moved it four miles south to a third-floor apartment on Spring Garden Street.

To commemorate their union, Joe set up his camera and pointed it at the kitchen table.

With his right foot he squeezed a bulb that triggered the shutter.

The Bohemians

MAM: *We went to the art store. I spent forty dollars.*

KID: *Such extravagance.*

MAM: *I guess I've got enough supplies for the rest of my life. But you know, I just enjoy painting so much.*

PAD: *Mammy bought a stretched canvas.*

KID: *Really! Not just a little canvas panel?*

MAM: *I wanted a bigger canvas for that vase I bought when you took us shopping last time. Of course, I may be dead before I ever finish the one I'm working on now. But at least the canvas won't go to waste. Pad can always use it.*

PAD: *I would like to have taken her picture. She looked beautiful.*

MAM: *I looked what?*

PAD: *Beautiful.*

MAM: *Me? Creeping along, dragging myself by sheer will power?*

PAD: *There was a good picture in it, though. Cane in one hand. Big white bag with a stretched canvas in the other.*

MAM: *Who'd want to look at that? I'm glad you didn't have the camera.*

PAD: *Believe me, there was a good picture in it.*

I

Based on their work at the Graphic Sketch Club, Joe and Irene were both offered scholarships to the top local art schools.

Joe was invited to Tyler School of Fine Arts. "But it was a kind of ritzy place. Everything was so clean. Not like the Graphic Sketch Club—there the paint was splattered all over the floor. And at Tyler you'd have to *study*, too!" So he declined.

Mam got her invitation to Moore College of Art, the preeminent women's institution. "I went down a few nights, but it wasn't for me. I don't think I even did them the courtesy of telling them I was turning down their scholarship. I still feel bad about that."

In other words: they knew that if they went their separate ways, they'd lose the romance of it all.

II

I was reading yesterday's newspaper at the big oval kitchen table with its Princess-and-the-Pea flannel-backed plastic tablecloths. It was very quiet, the kitchen TV being off. My parents regard television as an intoxication never to be imbibed before late afternoon.

Pad rattled the pots and pans in the cupboard at the far end of the room. "How about some pancakes?" he said, seductively brandishing a square Teflon griddle.

"Yes, please."

"Then you make 'em. I'll teach you how."

I joined Pad at the L-shaped avocado-green counter. And here he taught me to make pancakes exactly as he makes them every Saturday morning.

JOE TELLER PANCAKES

1. Heat your flaking Teflon griddle over the low blue flame of an avocado-green gas stove, vintage 1970.

2. Toss together in a saucepan warped from no less than thirty years' use:

> 1 cup white flour (stored in a coffee jar)
> 1 cup wheat flour (ditto)
> 1 tablespoon baking powder (a real tablespoon right out of the drawer, not an effete measuring spoon)
> ½ tablespoon baking soda (stick the big spoon into the box and bring it out half full. Don't worry about spilling baking soda; it helps keep roaches away.)
> The right amount of cinnamon (shake it from a large bottle until you can imagine Pad saying, "Okay, that's enough.")

3. Now, in another pan that has long deserved requiem, mix three eggs, two cups of milk, and a couple of tablespoons of oil. Beat until "nice and foamy" with an incredibly durable electric mixer you got as a drug-store premium. Combine the nice and foamy stuff with the dry, and there's your batter.

Now the entertainment begins.

"First," said Pad, "you got to feed yourself. You can't make pancakes for anybody else if you're hungry. Use two tablespoons of batter for each pancake."

I did, then served us the hot-off-the-griddle pancakes drenched with mellowed fresh fruit cup from a big bowl in the fridge.

"Now you do the art pancake for yo' Mammy. You dribble the batter on and it makes shapes. It always looks like something. Attaboy! What does it look like to you?"

"Um, that part could be a heron..."

"And this part could be a tadpole," he said, "and over here, there's a baby coming right out of the mother."

I tried not to perform a cesarean as I flipped the pancake.

Just then, Mam walked in, freshly showered and rouged, dressed in slacks and a flowered blouse with a gold wreath pin at the neck. Pad poured hot water onto the instant coffee in her cup. "Such service!" she exclaimed.

As Mam reached for her spoon, she paused and looked at her hand and said, not sadly but with a sort of detached fascination, rather like a paleontologist observing a fossilized trilobite, "Did you ever see anything more grotesque than that hand? Look at the veins!"

Pad said, "Well, no wonder. You're as old as the hills. You're practically dead."

That got Mam laughing. Tellers love death jokes.

"I'm tired of making pancakes," Pad said. "You finish up the batter and put the extras in the ice-a-box. Later you can stick 'em in the toaster for snacks. I'm going out for today's paper."

He left. He was happy. He had taught his kid to cook and had made his wife laugh.

"I swear," said Mam, after he was out of earshot, "on his deathbed, he will be kidding the nurse."

I put the plate with the art pancake in front of her. She studied the meandering blob of cooked batter.

"How did you do that?" she exclaimed. "It's a perfect camel!"

III

Pad returned with the newspaper. He put on his high-power reading glasses and hunched over the kitchen table to do his daily Jumble puzzle. He is so expert that he works in ink.

Mam had eaten up to the rear hump of her art pancake. "When we lived up at Spring Garden Street, we had a canary that would fly over and sit on the edge of your plate and eat your eggs."

"Rather cannibalistic," I said. "How'd he get out of the cage?"

"We left the door open all the time," said Pad.

"Joe's father gave us a beautiful bookcase. A big, ornate, hand-carved wooden cabinet. The canary loved to perch on top of it."

"So it was all decorated with bird dirt," said Pad. He returned to his puzzle.

"I remember walking up the stairs and spotting a rat *this big* right behind me. I hopped on Joe's back."

"You were what they call 'bohemians.' "

"No, we were what you call 'poor.' I used to go downstairs and buy twenty-five cents' worth of vegetables, and that's what we'd have to eat."

"We went for a walk in Fairmount Park one night," said Pad. "It was snowy. And this cat kept following us. She was obviously pregnant. So we took her home and put her in a drawer of the filing cabinet. The next morning we woke up and there were five kittens. We kept them in the bathtub."

"When they were old enough, I took one in to the Colonnade, and suddenly everyone there wanted a kitten. So we had our bathtub back."

Pad held up his puzzle. "I've got it. The clue is, 'What they served in the insane asylum,' and the drawing shows crazy people in a cafeteria line." He paused for effect. " 'SOUP TO NUTS.' "

IV

PAD: *Here's your pancake. What is it?*

MAM: *Well, I don't see anything right off. All I can get is…um…a squatting frog. I have to say it's not one of your best.*

PAD: *I know. I should've thinned the batter and let it dribble more. Come on, eat your pancake.*

MAM: *I'm not hungry, Joe.*

PAD: *That's because you don't like the design.*

MAM: *You're probably right. I'd probably eat it if it attracted me. But a squatting frog…*

In December 1939 the Colonnade cafeteria needed seasonal decorations, and Irene suggested holiday-themed paintings. In fact, she said, her husband could paint them to order.

"It was six paintings," said Mam, "about seven by eight feet. Big enough to cover the windows in the restaurant—of course they were fake windows—the restaurant was on the basement level."

"I tacked cheap muslin up on the wall by our bed and knocked them out in an hour or two apiece. We couldn't afford much paint, so I thinned it all out with turpentine. There was one with cowboys in the snow. And an angel where Mammy modeled for the hands…"

"And I remember a French woman came into the restaurant and saw the paintings and said, 'Too much! Too much!' Can you imagine? The nerve!"

"What did we get for them? Five dollars each?"

"Fifty dollars for the whole set. So that fifty dollars was like—what do they call it when they put blood into you?"

"A transfusion?" I offered.

"That's it, a transfusion," she said. "They're still around here some-place, rolled up."

"No, I cut them up and put them out in the trash a couple of years ago," said Pad.

"Do me a favor," I said, "and don't go cutting up any more paint-ings, even cheap ones."

At the Spring Garden Street apartment, amongst rats, cats, and canaries, Joe began drawing his cartoons.

He knew that if he were to become a professional cartoonist, he'd have to turn out drawings five, six, maybe seven days a week. So he tested himself by doing one a day.

"I was working half-days as a copyboy at the *Inquirer*."

"Eva got you the job," Mam interjected.

"They'd yell, 'Hey, Teller, take this down to Editorial!' and I'd run it down. Then after work I'd go downtown and walk around all afternoon and get an idea for my cartoon. "I didn't make sketches. I just kept it all in my head, then I'd come home and sit down and draw."

The bookies used to meet at the flower stand.

"Trust me, dear, strychnine is a hundred percent undetectable in raspberry."

"Would you take thirty-eight cents and a newt?"

"I'd get your soup, only my wife's serving it."

"I'd sold the paintings to the Colonnade," said Mam. "So I thought I could sell the cartoons to the *Inquirer.*"

"She was my agent."

"Some agent! I don't know where I got the nerve. I marched right up to the editor in chief and plunked down the portfolio and told him to hire you. And he liked the cartoons, he really did. But there were no vacancies on the funny page."

"Gimme a Mack truck and I'll drive it right up Hitler's axis."

The rejection from the *Inquirer* was a blow, especially since the artist was a married man now, with rent to pay. But a close pal told Joe that "lettering men," commercial artists who drew the headlines for print advertisements, were in demand. Accustomed to rolling with the punches and determined to earn a living by the stroke of his brush, Joe put aside the portfolio full of cartoons and learned to turn rough pencil sketches into eye-catching headlines.

His pal was right. Lettering was a good business. Before long Joe had ad agencies all over town using his work.

Then Japan inconsiderately decided to bomb Pearl Harbor.

> PAD: *It's a cat with boxing gloves.*
> MAM: *I see a person's rear end with two bent-up legs. No, wait. Two swans talking. Talking really closely. Well, they're not slim swans. They're old feeble swans. And they're talking very closely; their heads are melting together.*
> PAD: *It's a squirrel with a cape.*

"I'll give you a penny for chewing gum, but if that won't quiet you,
I'll lock you in the concentration camp when we get home."

The War Trunk

*Mam set a red-and-yellow box of Royal Instant Lemon
Pudding Mix on the kitchen table. On the front was the
phrase HOWDY DOODY'S FAVORITE.*

"I bought that forty-five years ago," she said.
*I picked it up. On the back of the box was a color-it-your-
self trading card of Howdy Doody in his trademark
neckerchief and cowboy boots.*
The box was empty.
*Mam said, "I found it the other day in the bottom of that
big pot where I keep all the Jell-O and pudding. I
served it to Pad. I didn't tell him."*
"You served him forty-five-year-old pudding?"
*"It was perfectly good. I saved the box for you. It might be
worth something someday."*

I

Pad still takes his responsibilities as a married man seriously. Every
morning Mam writes him a shopping list, and he goes out on his
hunter-gatherer hike. He brings home the food, art supplies, and a
Philadelphia Inquirer. He doesn't hold a grudge.

One ice-coated February 13th I accompanied him on his morning
expedition. I spotted some irises among the flowers at Jin's Vegetable

Market. My mother loves the rich blue-purple of irises. It being the day before Valentine's Day, I ran in and bought the bouquet. It cost $6.95.

"Six-ninety-five for that little thing?" exclaimed Pad. "You better not let Mammy know what you paid for them."

"The only person who can bust me is *you*."

"Oh. That's right." He thought for a minute. "We'll say they were a dollar-ninety-five. I paid the dollar and you paid the ninety-five cents."

We stuck to our story and she was delighted, especially since the flowers were more than a token of affection. They were a bargain.

II

"You know what you should show him, Joe?" said Mam, cutting the stems of the flowers on the drain board.

"No, what?"

"The war trunk."

"You'd like that," said Pad to me. "It's *full* of old crap."

The "war trunk" was a footlocker in the cellar. It was buried under a broken toaster oven and seventy pounds of ceramic tile. Its lock was sealed shut by strips of brittle masking tape.

I ripped off the tape and lifted the lid. Everything inside was sprinkled with the dried turds of mice who long ago opted for pleasanter lodgings.

We sifted the rodent excreta from the three cubic feet of the trunk's contents and carried our prizes upstairs.

Mam was sitting at the kitchen table, drinking coffee in defiance of her doctor's orders. "Oh, it tastes so *good*," she said.

I took out an envelope filled with tiny photographs. There was Joe in his army uniform in front of a barracks.

"You were drafted, right?" I asked.

"I don't volunteer for anything."

"That's you at Camp Hahn, out in Riverside, California," said Mam. "That's where they taught you to be a telephone operator."

"No, Camp Hahn was basic training. That's where you wiggle under barbed wire while they shoot at you."

Another picture showed Joe standing by a road sign in the desert. "That was our day off," he said. "They gave us a day off in Death Valley! Nothing but peanut-butter-jelly sandwiches and a canteen of water, because anything else would spoil in that heat. That was our TREAT!"

"And I was in Philadelphia and got so sick of people commiserating with me about Joe being away that I took a train to California. Everybody was going off to war. The train was so long it extended beyond the platform.

"I was in there for four or five days, windows wide open with soot pouring in. When I got to Riverside, I went in to meet the woman who interviewed wives who needed jobs. She said, 'Your face is filthy. Why didn't you go wash up in the train bathroom before you arrived?' I said, 'What bathroom?' There was only one toilet on the whole train."

Irene got a job at a cafeteria and a free room in the hotel upstairs. "And I used to visit her," said Pad. "I'd stay there till four o'clock in the morning. Then the bus would take me and the other men visiting their wives back to the base. But we had to get up at five, so I'd barely get to sleep before I had to get right up. I remember the sergeant looking at me and yelling, 'Jeezuscrist, Teller, you shitfaced again?'"

Among the papers from the war trunk was an invitation for Irene to join the Camp Hahn Chaperones for tea. "Throw it away," she said. "I don't think I'll go."

III

Joe was transferred to Camp Polk, Louisiana. Irene followed.

I handed Mam the ledger she had kept as manager of the servicemen's club restaurant there. "Look at this," she said. "A day's worth of groceries for two-hundred-seventy dollars. No wonder the boss loved me. I was cheap."

"So," said Pad, "after they'd given us all that desert training—how to survive in the sun with no water—they shipped us to the Philippines for monsoon season."

"*He* had been a tramp," said Mam. "So living in a swamped-out tent in the same clothes week after week wasn't as much of a shock to him as it was to the other men. Only thing he couldn't stand was one loud-mouth who annoyed the whole camp. You fought with him, didn't you?"

Sweet, innocent voice: "No. Not me. I never fight with nobody."

"Yes you did!"

"Oh, you mean the Polish guy from Chicago? Well, I finally had to bump him on the head and knock him out. When you get hit on the top of the head with a fist, that knocks the brains out, just like a black-jack. He was all right after that."

"The whole time he was overseas I stayed in Camp Polk," said Mam. "I used to save chocolate bars to send to him. The smell enticed fire ants into my apartment. And all of a sudden in the middle of the night they were eating my legs. They wanted flesh. I'd never lived in Louisiana before. I had never *heard* of such a thing."

"Look at this," said Pad, handing me a photo of a hillside on which the word CORREGIDOR was written in white stones. "We were stationed on another island, and they gave us a day off and offered us a trip to Corregidor. They took us on a tour. They drove us around and showed us all the dead Japs in the caves. That was our fun. Another TREAT!"

IV

#228, January 10, 1946

Dear Irene,

Now, look, sweetie, please don't pay any attention to the following prediction, as it's all my own, but I'll be terribly disappointed if I ain't out of here by the end of January, which is what I said last month.

I tell you we keep listening for news on the radio just like we used to listen to the draft news at the beginning of the war. You know you're going, but you don't know when. Ain't it awful? Boy, I betcha when I get home I'm going to be a terrible stickler for promptness. As if I always wasn't anyway.

How are you getting along now? I take it for granted you've left Camp Polk by now and that you're in Philly, according to Eva's letter. Now, be very careful about the weather and please don't catch cold or get your feet wet or

nothing like that. Remember you just came from a
comparatively warm climate. When I get back I'll
probably have the shivers all day long, but won't I love it!
I hope you keep nice and warm and drink lots of hot cocoa
before you go to bed and snuggle in under two blankets
and a comforter and wear your little woolen booties and a
wool night cap when you go to bed. And don't forget your
heavy flannel nightgown and two pair of snuggies. Oh,
boy! Won't that feel good, though? Take good care of your-
self, my sweetie. I love you.

Joe

Last among the stuff we had brought up from the trunk was a three-inch cubical powder-blue gift box. It was tied shut with a red ribbon. I slid the ribbon off (it was so stiff it retained the square shape even when nothing was inside it) and opened the box. In it was a sheet of Jefferson Hospital stationery with my birth date and two infant footprints in ink. There was an envelope containing blondish-brown hair and a blue-and-white baby identification bracelet not much larger than a finger ring.

Joe and Irene had become Pad and Mam.

V

Loose in the bottom of that gift box was a single dried bean.

"That's a Mexican jumping bean. What's it doing there?" said Mam. She examined it. "Yes, that's exactly what it is, a Mexican jumping bean. They have a worm inside, you know; that's what makes it jump. But this one's not jumping. The worm must be dead."

"Oh, that worm is long since dead," said Pad.

I laughed. The worm was long since dead. It certainly was. We had pried our way into that fifty-year-old trunk and disturbed the leavings of mice from President Truman's day, so yes, indeed, that worm was very dead. The more I thought, "That worm is long since dead," the more I laughed. Mam caught the giggles from me, and then, probably because both his wife and kid were guffawing, Pad succumbed.

We calmed for a moment, then I croaked out, "THAT WORM IS LONG SINCE DEAD," and the cycle started all over.

So there we sat, all of us: Irene, Joe, Mam, Pad, and their prying Kid, there at the kitchen table where all matters of moment are unfolded, the Teller family laughing together like lunatics, our faces dripping with tears at a dried-up jumping bean and a worm long since dead.

DEAR IRENE:
YOUR TABLE MANNERS ARE
UNIQUE
YOU DON'T EAT NUTTIN' WHEN YOU
SPEAK

WITH HAPPINESS YOU FILL MY
LIFE
BECAUSE YOU'RE SUCH A LOVING
WIFE

TO SAVE MYSELF A MIGHTY
DOLLAR

I MADE THIS CARD SO YOU WONT
HOLLAR

HAPPY BIRTHDAY WITH
KISSES
                    Joe

Epilogue

PAD: *I went out today and there was the most beautiful sky. It rained yesterday and everything was so clean. I had my new shoes on, and I just stopped and looked up at the sky. I thought that if I stood there and looked up for a while, people would come and look up, too, to see what I was looking at. But I didn't get any customers.*

MAM: *It's a shame, isn't it. People don't look up at the sky, and it's about the most beautiful thing there is.*

PAD: *Gotta get a good look at where I'm going any day now.*

MAM: *Oh, shoot! I'm going to get burned up.*

PAD: *You should get a ride on that comet. What's its name?*

MAM: *I can never think of it.*

KID: *Hale-Bopp?*

PAD: *Yup. That'd be a nice ride, all right.*

As a home for the Kid, Pad and Mam bought a high-ceilinged Lincoln-era row house in the middle of Philadelphia. Pad worked long hours, hunched over the drafting table in the top-floor studio, where he shaped words with surgical precision in India ink. Commercial art and fatherhood were Pad's jobs now. But somehow he always managed to keep an oil painting in progress on his easel and a prism by his palette for inspiration.

He never tried to sell his paintings. After all, as he says, nobody ever made a living at fine art.

And the cartoons? They waited patiently in the grimy black portfolio for sixty years, quietly laughing at themselves.

> MAM [a thrill in her voice]: *Published? The cartoons?*
> *You mean in a book? With Pad's name on it?*
> KID: *That's what I said.*
> MAM [pause, skeptical]: *What does it cost us?*
> KID: *It doesn't cost us anything. Stores sell the book.*
> *People buy it. Pad gets paid.*
> MAM: *I can't believe it! What an honor…after all these*
> *years.*
> PAD: *Honor, schmonor! Let's go sell some paintings!*

Edited by
T. Gene Hatcher
and
Laura Lindgren & Ken Swezey

The author gratefully declares that the above-named
highly demanding and inspiring people were full creative partners
in the composition of this book.

The cover photos were taken by Bill Cramer, Philadelphia.
Interior art photography by Scott Lindgren, Los Angeles.

Additional informative, witty, and artistic suggestions from:
Colman deKay
and
Ray Beiersdorfer, Celia Fuller, Heidi Glassman-Gonzales,
Michael Goudeau, Tammy Hulfachor, Penn Jillette, Don Kennison,
Robert P. Libbon, Ken Siman, Colin Summers, Arne Svenson

And thanks to:
Glenn Alai, Tom Gundy, Kenneth Lewis,
Eleanor Reynolds, Dan Strone, Gretchen Worden

And, of course,

Joe & Irene Teller

photo by Kid, c. 1958